When Homeschooling Gets Tough
by Diana Johnson

When Homeschooling Gets Tough
Published by Home-Designed Schooling
P.O. Box 133044
Tyler, TX 75713-3044
Copyright © 2003 by Diana Johnson
All Rights Reserved
ISBN 0-9710734-1-4

Available through
your local Christian bookstore
and homeschool catalogs,
or contact
homedesignedschooling@cox-internet.com
or
homeschool@thescroll.org

*Dedicated with special thanks to
my husband John
for his heartfelt reminders
to always use my writing
to point to Christ*

Contents

Preface

Welcome! Thank you for picking up this book. I wonder what drew you to it. Author name recognition? I don't think so. Delightful cover art? As I write these words no cover yet exists. Past history tells me it will be okay, but it won't be the ultimate eye candy. It must have been the title! *When Homeschooling Gets Tough*. Notice the title is not, *If Homeschooling Gets Tough*. After twenty years of directing our humble little school, I assure you that *when* is the correct word here.

Unfortunately, homeschoolers don't always talk about that: at least, not often enough. We prefer to discuss the glowing moments, while breathing collective maternal sighs of delight. Those wonderful moments do exist. We're not making them up. But other moments exist, too. That's what the ladies at the secluded back table were whispering about at last month's support group meeting. We heard plenty of laughter, but I believe there were some tears, too.

That's what this book is all about: those *other* moments, which sometimes seem to vastly outnumber the glowing moments. As I've written, I've tried to be honest with you. That honesty requires some straightforward talk. Homeschooling *is* hard. Sometimes it's very hard. But it's good, honest kingdom work for the Lord, and the eternal blessings can be great indeed.

May this book be a companion for your hard times. May its honesty be an arm of comfort around your shoulder. May it give you hope in the struggle. May it remind you how much the Savior loves you!

Because we are precious in His sight,
Diana Johnson

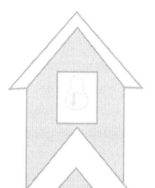

"Rufus was so happy he was going to start school, his face was shining."

The Moffats by Eleanor Estes

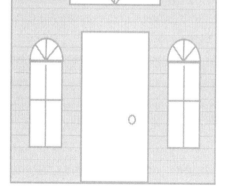

Our Homeschool Odyssey

I have always loved school. I loved new pencil cases, paper, and books. I loved how they smelled! I loved the crisp fall weather that accompanied the new school year in my midwestern childhood home. If it hadn't been for the winter mornings that began before daylight, I could have stayed in elementary school for the rest of my life. I actually tried to. Moving south, I attended a fine Christian university where I chose elementary education as my major. I enjoyed a short teaching career before settling down to marriage and motherhood. My kindergartners and second graders loved me. I loved them. My southern students with gentle accents were learning to read under a teacher with the nasality of a Chicagoan.

The September when my oldest son was born, I went back to school with everyone else, but not to teach. Instead I squeaked in a few weeks of after school daycare before I became a mother. It was the closest I could get to a classroom in my rotund condition. Much to the fear and consternation of my principal, I persuaded my daycare replacement to let me work a few weeks beyond our agreed switchover time. I quit just shy of my first labor pains. The surface reason was to afford the rocking chair that still graces our living room. The real reason was that I had to go back to school.

The first autumn I couldn't go back to school was a hard one. My husband was in seminary and working two jobs so I could stay home with the baby. We didn't see much of each other. As I recall, I did some tutoring and babysitting to supplement our income, but it wasn't the same. I still remember looking out the window of our duplex, yearning after the school bus lumbering down our street.

My husband graduated from seminary and we took our first church call. That winter he came home from an out of town conference where he had the happy opportunity to visit with some old seminary friends. And guess what? They were homeschooling!

I still remember looking out the window of our duplex, yearning after the school bus lumbering down our street.

My husband thought it was a great idea. I thought he was crazy. During this time our oldest, (there were now two children) was going through some fairly extensive testing. Something just wasn't right. That something turned out to be a significant hearing loss. At four he was fitted with his first hearing aids, which brought his hearing much closer to normal ranges. It was a time of adventure. Did you know that crickets chirp? Did you know that leaves crunch when you step on them? I remember a mom in similar circumstances sharing her daughter's ecstatic comments when she got her first glasses, "Mommy, look! Trees have leaves!"

Our son was enrolled in a public school speech and language development class. His teacher was a

Christian, welcomed us into the classroom, and ate in our home. Each Monday morning she would guide the children in writing a dictated story about their weekend. Their Sunday church activities were prominently highlighted. Why homeschool?

The next year we moved from the promised land back to Egypt. The kindergarten teacher had more than 60 students between her two kindergarten sessions and could not keep tabs on the children as individuals. Our son was miserable walking alone to speech therapy. In his opinion it was a glaring testimony that he was a misfit. The new kindergartners needing speech were caught in the slow school bureaucracy and would not start their therapy for months.

None of this persuaded me to homeschool. The defining moment didn't come until my first parent-teacher conference. I sat down at a little kindergartner's desk across from the teacher, both of our knees almost to our chins as we sat in the little chairs. She was not impressed that I had been a kindergarten teacher. There were no comradely feelings. There were no *aren't these little ones wonderful* comments. She shared my son's aptitude test, pointing out his errors. It seems he was asked, "What do you put on when you dance?" The answer was music. He said clothes. It worked for me. She said it was wrong.

The real clincher that finally tipped me into homeschooling came at the end of conference. She did not ask if I had any questions. I wanted to discuss my marvelous son. She did not. Rather, the teacher abruptly stood to dismiss me. I was tempted to keep myself glued to the chair and see what she would do. But I didn't. She was too intimidating. My reluctance had finally been conquered, and soon after we began to homeschool.

Twenty years and twelve grades later, all taught several times over, we are still attempting the challenge. By the time we finish, Lord willing, we will have homeschooled 28 years. I'm hopeful I will get a gold watch upon my retirement, suitably engraved, "Barring algebra, she stood undaunted."

About six years into our homeschool adventure our local homeschool group asked my husband to take over its leadership. At the same time our public library requested that we give homeschool seminars in their adult informational program. At these seminars we would often suggest homeschool books that our audience could read for further information. Thus, our relationship with the Scroll Christian Bookstore began. David Rooker, the manager, was happy to accommodate us by stocking the books we requested.

A few years into this beneficial arrangement, David casually shared with my husband a desire to expand the few shelves of homeschool books into a full-fledged department. He just needed to find someone to help him. Very pregnant with my fifth, I asked David if I could volunteer some time to help. The adventure began soon after little Hannah was born. My interest was not totally altruistic. Between my education background and my years of homeschooling, I was a curriculum lover. Selfishly, I wanted to bring products in that I knew were good and bless my own little homeschool in the process.

It has been ten years since department discussions began. Time has changed a volunteer activity (a couple of hours a week during baby's naptime) into an incredibly busy full time summer job and a more controlled part time job during the school year. I have learned a lot during these years.

Teaching my children has been a time of learning for our whole family. My five children, Brian, Cara, John Aaron, Grace, and Hannah, have taught me more than I have taught them. How much we learn about ourselves when we homeschool!

Working in the bookstore has also grown me up. Interacting with customers, reviewing, ordering, studying, and explaining curriculum has been a phenomenal learning experience. Both my personal homeschool and the homeschool department at the Scroll have been a labor of love.

As you read the following pages, don't assume I have all the answers or that my homeschool exemplifies the best way to school. I struggle like you. Sometimes I do it right and I rejoice. Sometimes I do it wrong and I try to learn from the mistake.

Occasionally you may feel that I am tweaking your nose a little, issuing a gentle rebuke. Don't feel bad, I have tweaked my own nose plenty as I've written this! Although we all acknowledge our call to obedience and holiness, the real desire of my heart is that we recognize the impossibility of achieving such perfection here and now. May we enjoy a growing peace and patience towards each other and ourselves as we trust our final perfection in eternity to the Lord's redeeming work.

Many of my homeschool thoughts and ideas come from my frequent interaction with homeschool friends and customers. I have been invited to peek into the homeschool lives of innumerable people through casual visits enjoyed in the aisles of the homeschool department. It has expanded my knowledge greatly and I am thankful. I hope it has made me wiser.

I will praise You, for I am fearfully and wonderfully made; Marvelous are Your works, and that my soul knows very well. (Psalm 139:14)

How precious also are Your thoughts to me, O God! How great is the sum of them! If I should count them, they would be more in number than the sand. (Psalm 139:17,18a)

Trusting God for Who We Are

Managing the homeschool department of a bookstore means constant discussions on curriculum, children, and their individual learning needs. Some of the moms I meet are upbeat and confident about themselves, their children, and the path they have chosen. Others are unsure of themselves, defeated, and fearful they are doing an awful job. Where are you? Perhaps you can be in both places on the same day depending on the subject you teach.

By the time this book comes out, I will be in my 20th year of homeschooling. I have graduated three students successfully. The two students left are progressing well. Illiteracy has never cast a threatening shadow over our doorway. Even in math, our weakest area, our children will survive, provided algebra doesn't intrude into their lives too regularly.

Yet I find myself regularly filled with self-doubt. Sometimes this happens while I am speaking to a soft-spoken mother with a gentle demeanor. Her quiet voice casts clouds of grace around each sweet duckling following her about the aisles of the store. My mind will wander: *Oh, I was too harsh with Hannah this morning. Why can't I be as gentle as this mom?* Or it may be the mom who confidently teaches advanced math and does, not just any old science experiments, but advanced labs, *real* labs, with microscopes and detailed reports. Wow! Now my mind wanders in different directions: *The hardest experiment we've ever done is sticking celery stalks in colored water. Maybe Cara wouldn't have changed her mind about studying nursing if I had done a better job like this mom.*

The hardest experiment we've ever done is sticking celery stalks in colored water.

As homeschool moms we sometimes look at others and draw comparisons for who we should be and where we are lacking. We look at one person and desire her sweetness of character; we look at another and admire her personal discipline and organization, yet another her intellectual abilities, another her dress size or looks, and on and on it goes. We meld these characteristics into one super homeschool mom, unconsciously assuming she exists—but not in us. As if these self-condemning thoughts aren't enough, sometimes the homeschool books, magazines, seminars, and mom's meetings meant to comfort and inspire leave us with more feelings of guilt and defeat. *I'm not like them. I'm not as disciplined. Our home isn't as godly. I'm an ineffective, muddled mess.*

How do we change our perspective? How do we find victory over our thoughts? Contentment lies in accepting that God in His wisdom has made our family who we are. It means accepting ourselves and our teaching style, our husband's level of involvement in our homeschool, and our children's accomplishments. It means recognizing our worth in Christ.

Be Content with Yourself and Your Teaching Style

Who are we? We are women, wives, mothers, friends—and homeschool teachers. Because of the commitment involved and the seriousness of the task, sometimes, perhaps most of the time, the homeschool part of our identity seems to loom larger than everything else. It is an area where we often feel great vulnerability and self-doubt, where we are quick to observe and compare ourselves with others. We don't always like what we see.

Scripture teaches us, as Christians, to be content with our placement in the body of Christ. We are urged not to compare our position unfavorably with that of others. We read in I Corinthians 12:14-19:

> *For in fact the body is not one member but many. If the foot should say, "Because I am not a hand, I am not of the body," is it therefore not of the body? And if the ear should say, "Because I am not an eye, I am not of the body," is it therefore not of the body? If the whole body were an eye, where would be the hearing? If the whole were hearing, where would be the smelling? But now God has set the members, each one of them, in the body **just as He pleased**. And if they were all one member, where would the body be?* [emphasis added]

As homeschoolers, we have diverse roles in this area of God's kingdom work. We will run our schools very differently from each other. We will hold to different philosophies, choose different methodologies, follow different schedules, and place great importance on different subjects. Meaning no irreverence for the Word of God, I would like to make a respectful application of I Corinthians 12:14-19 to homeschooling choices:

> *For, in fact, the homeschool community is not one schooling model, but many. If the textbook user should say, "Because I don't use unit studies, I'm not a good homeschooler," is she therefore not a good homeschooler? And if the living book user should say, "Because I haven't tested my fourth grader at all this year, I am not a good homeschooler," is she therefore not a good homeschooler? If everyone had to use textbooks for everything, what would happen to the child who devours literature and loves wordplay and will turn that love into a creative writing or teaching career that honors God? If everyone had to use unit studies, what would happen to the child who really, truly, loves workbooks and will carry that love for order into a successful, God-honoring law or business career? But now God has given us all individual interests and abilities **just as He pleased**. And if we were all carbon copies of each*

other, what would happen to our ability to diversely and wonderfully bring glory to God?

After homeschooling 20 years, you would think I would be settled and sure of myself. Actually, I find it humorous how, in the course of a busy, get-ready-for-homeschool, summer workday, I can find my thoughts spinning with all the good ideas I hear from my knowledgeable customers. *Maybe I should consider that curriculum for this coming school year? That's a wonderful activity they are involved in. Maybe we should do it, too?* Finding out who I am and my homeschool identity is still an ongoing activity!

As we wrestle with our homeschool identities, there are some assurances in which we can rest. We know God has fashioned us as He intended us to be. We know He desires us to be faithful and obedient in our unique abilities, struggles, and circumstances. And we know we are precious to Him.

Be Content with Your Husband's Involvement

"As my husband was leading our family devotions the other day..." "I don't teach math and science, my husband does that." "My husband watches the kids each Saturday so I can get the next week's school preparation done." "My husband hired a babysitter and surprised me with a weekend away."

Have you ever made one of those statements, or one similar? How blessed you are! Be thankful!

Perhaps you have heard such statements made, knowing they didn't represent your situation. You might have felt tired inside, trying to feel happy for the blessings of another, but not entirely succeeding. Welcome back to the dismal world of comparisons!

My husband has pastored the same small church for twenty years. He is dedicated to that task. The people are his lambs and he loves them deeply. His caring takes him to scout activities, plays, and concerts of our church youth. He knows the joy of the hospital nursery and the anxiety of the emergency room. He could walk the hospital corridors blindfolded. He shares in the sorrow of hospice, accompanying family members to the funeral home to pick out a casket and make final arrangements for their loved one. He is a hand holder and hand patter as people go through the joys and struggles of life.

He preaches each Sunday. He labors over his messages. After services he greets his people warmly. His suit shoulders often have makeup on them (not mine) and baby drool. He loves the little ones and greets them as sincerely as he greets their parents. He is regularly seen with a child in his arms.

Guess what? He doesn't teach math in our homeschool. He doesn't teach science either. Even family devotions can be crowded out if church needs or responsibilities are too pressing. It happens more often than either of us would like to admit.

There have been times in the past when I devoured too many homeschool books or was enraptured by too many homeschool presentations. Right before my very eyes I would see homeschool dads who seemed to personify perfect homeschool manhood. They were always there for heart-to-hearts with mom or kids, to guide, direct, and discipline when it was needed. I would find myself becoming very ideal-

Casting my eyes on my beloved, I would find him sorely wanting.

istic and grumpy. Casting my eyes on my beloved, I would find him sorely wanting.

How do we learn satisfaction with the homeschool dads God has given us? When I am tempted to think my husband is not comparing favorably to another homeschool dad, I remind myself of two things. First of all, no homeschool dad is perfect. Regardless of what I think my eyes see or think my ears hear, I know that it is the common lot of redeemed sinners to walk an uneven walk this side of heaven. The Bible makes this clear. We are all striving to glorify God through our individual family situations. It is a struggle for everyone. To be honest, some have greater struggles than others, but it is Christ who strengthens us all.

Secondly, although my husband and I are both committed to our family and to homeschooling, we live it out differently. My daily activities are full of meeting family needs, hands-on and directly. For a large portion of each day homeschooling is uppermost in my mind, the center of my thoughts and energies. Since my husband's livelihood does not come from a homeschooling business, homeschooling is not at the top of his daily priority list. By necessity his thoughts are much more divided. The work realm consumes much of his thought, time, and energy. These work activities put food on our table, clothes on our back, a warm shelter over our heads, and make homeschooling possible.

In addition, my husband cares about our schooling. He shows this in quiet, non-dramatic ways. He frees up my time to homeschool by assisting in household tasks. He is patient with my meandering discussions of curriculum options. He listens attentively when I discuss a child's academic struggles. When asked, he will thoughtfully render judgment on schooling decisions over which I am struggling. It is enough.

Perhaps your husband plays an active role in your homeschool. Perhaps he leaves it all to you. Whatever our individual situations may be, it does not honor God to pressure our husbands to conform to our expectations. As wives, we are to be helpmeets. We are to have a servant's heart.

Proverbs 31:10-12 reminds us: "Who can find a virtuous wife? For her worth is far above rubies. The heart of her husband safely trusts her; so he will have no lack of gain. She does him good and not evil all the days of her life."

Our husbands are not delinquent in their duties if they safely trust us to manage the homeschool part of our family's life. We should feel honored that they trust our judgment in an area so vital to their children's future. Life is so much bigger than homeschooling. May God direct our eyes to the other areas of life where our husbands bless us greatly, and may we be thankful.

Be Content with Your Children's Accomplishments

I have a coffee mug I recently purchased on vacation. The girl on the mug wears a frazzled look and equally frazzled hairdo. Her apt philosophical statement reads, "Life is just so daily." Children have a way of making us feel that way.

Daily spilled milk; daily sticky floors; daily math errors (the same mistakes to be repeated the next day); daily lost papers, books, and pencils; daily papers to grade; and daily quarreling. And the weeklies aren't much different. Weekly lessons to prepare, weekly music lessons to hurry to, and weekly missed appointments. Two of the most frequently spoken sentences at our home are, "Hurry, we're going to be late! You can put your shoes on in the car."

In addition to the inevitable "dailies" and "weeklies," there is another reality. There will always be children who are brighter, more poised, more obedient, more parent-honoring, and more handsome or beautiful than mine. In fact, my lofty dreams of my children's accomplishments and virtues would be amusing if I weren't so serious! I take comfort in knowing I'm not the only one who dreams. I remember a co-worker at the bookstore sharing with me a mom's matter-of-fact expectation that her child would be a National Merit Scholar. After all, they were homeschooling!

Unfortunately, there can be a problem with all that dreaming. Like the dreams of our sleep, they are usually larger than real life. They are not based on reality. We will dream of full tuition college scholarships when achievement tests show our children are scraping to hit grade level. We may dream of our son becoming an engineer while, despite continuous effort, the multiplication facts remain a mystery. We may dream of our daughter becoming a writer whose salient and gifted writing will influence the world for Christ, yet her dislike of reading is second only to her dislike of composition. Unfortunately, our children are quick to recognize when, sometimes through no fault of their own, they are shattering our misguided dreams. None of us, our children included, enjoys feelings of inadequacy. Even when our dreams *are* in harmony with our children's talents and abilities, our children sometimes surprise and disappoint us when they do not appreciate our carefully planned goals. Why doesn't my student understand what a good idea I have for him?

Unrealistic expectations can also be fueled by those around us. Grandma and grandpa have misgivings about our homeschooling, so we struggle to make each child a superior academic product. Friends at church or in the neighborhood have children winning honors in sports, academics, or fine arts at the local public or private schools. They ask, "How is your child doing?" We rack our brain for accomplishments and come up dry. Somehow the fact that our child's music teacher finds him well-mannered doesn't compare favorably.

Even within the homeschool community we can find ourselves unhappily comparing our children's accomplishments with those of others. As always, comparing leaves us discontented, perhaps even feeling sick inside. How do we escape the dreaded cycle of false expectations?

As always, comparing leaves us discontented, perhaps even feeling sick inside.

I would strongly caution you not to look for solace by disparaging the accomplishments of others. It is common in homeschooling circles to view accomplishments achieved in public school with suspicion. After all, the student is probably a closet rebel and got an award because he could at least read! I have been blessed to have these thoughts chastened out of me by two wonderful friends.

One friend is a homeschool mom, committed Christian, and part time public school counselor. She has watched Christian students excel in public school, rising to the challenge to be salt and light in a place Christ is not honored. The second friend is my younger sister. We have both cheered each other on, sharing the struggles and accomplishments of her three children in public school and my five in homeschool. Her oldest daughter is a godly, disciplined premed student, active in church and on mission trips—an honor to Christ.

Although by no means do I offer an endorsement of all that occurs in our public school system or recommend it as the best place for our Christian youth, I do recognize that by God's grace good things can happen regardless of schooling methods. Christian students in public school have a tremendous battle before them. I honor those who stand firm for the Lord against the odds. Battles for God's kingdom occur on all of life's fronts and they are most difficult where the lines are sparsely defended.

I would strongly urge you to develop deep relationships with a few honest friends. Seek out moms who share your faith in Christ, can truly rejoice when you rejoice, and are not afraid to stand in life's muck with you when necessary. In your church body, build relationships with older women who are wise in the Lord and able to encourage. Ask for their counsel and prayer support. Such friends who love your children and will pray for them with you are one of life's best blessings. Be a true prayer warrior for them and their families in return. It's amazing how we grow to love and care about those for whom we pray!

I would strongly encourage you to let God determine your dreams for your children. We cannot know in advance God's sovereign will for our children in specific detail. However, we do know it is always God's will for us to desire our children's spiritual growth. To dream of children that honor the Lord is profitable provided that the dream is accompanied by prayer! In addition, praying for open doors to specific career fields or for the development of our children's particular talents is also fine provided we sincerely mean "not my will, but Thine." This means being willing to abandon our dreams when they are clearly not God's direction. The best course is to humbly seek the face of God, children and parents together, asking for wisdom for the present and for the future. James 1:5 offers us excellent advice: "If any of you lacks wisdom, let him ask of God, who gives to all liberally and without reproach, and it will be given to him." God is not delinquent in guiding those who seek His glory.

Recognize Your Worth in Christ.

I love Psalm 139. It clearly speaks of God's individual interest in *me*. I *am* fearfully and wonderfully made, and so are my husband and my children. So are you and your family. God has made us all unique. We all have something special to offer. We all have great worth in Christ.

God grant us grace to turn our eyes away from unhealthy comparisons with others and toward Christ! This is where our genuine worth lies. I am deeply humbled and grateful when I read the words of John 17:20-21. His suffering and death looming, Jesus prays in the upper room:

*I do not pray for these alone, **but also for those who will believe in Me through their word;** that they all may be one, as You, Father, are in Me, and I in You, that they also may be one in Us, that the world may believe that You sent Me. [emphasis added]*

In that evening of deepest distress, His thoughts were on me! His thoughts were on you! His prayer for us is for oneness with fellow believers, with Him, and with the Father. Redeemed in Christ, we are truly engraved on the palms of His hands: a place of sheltered love and inexpressible worth. This is where our true well-being lies. May our most fervent prayers and expressions of gratitude rest in these higher eternal realities, not in the trenches of math problems and book reports.

change ling (chānj-lēn) n: an infant secretly exchanged for another by fairies, popular theme in folk tales. adj: A characteristic of homeschool curriculum in which unexpected changes occur overnight. <This changeling curriculum is driving me crazy!>

Johnson's Revised Dictionary of Unusual Terms

Planning a Realistic Program

My bedroom has a very large walk-in closet. I would love it to be filled with beautiful clothes, all wearable, preferably size eight. Instead it is filled with schoolbooks. One entire wall of floor to ceiling shelves is mostly filled with curriculum on inactive duty not quite ready for disposal. After all, I might need it for my two younger children. Quite a few stacked boxes handle the overflow, not to mention the books I've sold or given away! Bookcases of "real" or "living" books cover walls in every room of the house except the bathrooms. The dining area buffet long ago ousted the table linens and kitchenware from its shelves in favor of our current curriculum choices. Books have taken over our lives. My work in a book-store has only exacerbated the problem. A twenty year curriculum habit is a formidable problem, indeed!

The passage of time is not the only thing that has added to our curriculum overload. I am often an out-of-control perfectionist, wanting to teach my children each and every fact that could ever, even remotely, be of benefit to them. I rush to fill gaps, real or imagined, like the little boy hurrying to stick his finger in the breach of the dike. Perhaps you share my behavior? Add to finger-in-the-dike behavior a dedicated study of homeschool books, and the problem can really intensify. We become like a friend of Jane Lambert's (*Five in a Row*), quoted in Diana Waring's book *Things We Wish We'd Known*, "If a little is good, then more is better and too much is just right!"

We become engaged in a quest, an honorable pursuit of the perfect homeschool cur-

We become engaged in a quest, an honorable pursuit of the perfect homeschool curriculum.

riculum. We seriously examine our options, discarding our current choice when another promises to light a greater passion for learning in our children. Our children endure our constant changes in methodology. Like medieval knights, we lead our small band on a courageous crusade for the holy grail of curriculum choices.

Controlling the Curriculum Quest

We really do need to keep our curriculum quest in check. Our children need order and continuity, not constant change. Our husbands need to know we are not destroying the family budget with unnecessary homeschool purchases. How do we control our desire to constantly improve our curriculum?

First of all, come back to reality. Modify or abandon your honorable quest for homeschool perfection. I am very fond of telling my customers, "There is no such thing as the best. There is no perfect curriculum." I have been tempted to make some people write it ten times. When someone asks me, "What's the best?" any smart co-worker will leave rather than listen to me pontificate for the umpteenth time.

Curriculum all have unique personalities. So do parents and students. As a homeschool teacher your challenge is to smoothly mesh all three factors—the curriculum, teacher, and student personalities and needs—into a cohesive, workable program. The choices made and the results achieved will be different for every family.

One of the biggest mistakes first time homeschoolers can make is to assume that their homeschooling friend's great program is the right choice for them. (It doesn't help when their friend uses the word *best* when describing it!) I always encourage my customers to listen carefully to as many homeschooling friends as possible because their advice is truly invaluable. But each prospective homeschooler must evaluate this information through the sieve of some important questions: "Is my friend like me? Are our energy levels for preparation and creativity similar? Are her children like mine? Do they share common academic strengths and weaknesses? Is her family budget similar to ours?" Through this family evaluation the helpfulness of the advice increases. When your friends and their children are very different from yours, it will help you to view their curriculum as *possibly* being a wrong choice for you. If your friends and their children are similar to your family, perk up and listen more carefully. You may have found the help you need.

What if you are already a dedicated home-schooler, yet you find things are just not clicking anymore? Sometimes our circumstances change and what works well at one time no longer fits. A new baby arrives. A toddler graduates to formal education and needs the time we had been devoting to big brother. Instead of two students, we now have three. Instead of three students, we now have four. Instead of four students, we now have five. (It's getting scary, isn't it?) Perhaps our husband needs us to work part time in his business. These are just a few of the many life changes that can affect our homeschooling.

Life takes us through different seasons and the homeschool journey is part of that. A method which works well with our little ones may not be as appropriate as our children mature. We need to adapt our program to the age of our students and to the flow of life. Be cautious of being so tied to one homeschool philosophy that you cannot make changes when they are appropriate. Be cautious also of changing curriculum too quickly or too often.

Before making curriculum changes, I would encourage you to evaluate why something isn't working. Perhaps the program requires more preparation time than you have. Keeping up with the grading may be too formidable a challenge. The reading level may be too easy or too difficult for your student. In math, perhaps the concepts are explained abstractly, not providing your student with needed hands-on help. Whatever the difficulty, the better you can define the problem the more likely you will find a suitable solution.

Once you have defined the problem, start looking for a replacement that addresses the need. Check out your information sources: homeschool friends, books, the internet, catalogs, bookstores, conventions, etc. When you are ready to make a decision, you will have done all you can to insure its success.

I am fond of saying another phrase, "If it ain't broke, don't fix it." Sometimes we make changes just for the sake of change. I'm not saying this is wrong. At times a change is very refreshing. But constant change for no good reason, can lead to curriculum repetitions and gaps. Textbooks do not all follow the same order and timing in the presentation of skills. Changing programs without careful thought can be particularly detrimental in math, where a careful sequence of skills is necessary for mastery.

It is probably best to make changes slowly, subject by subject rather than across the board. This prevents a momentary enthusiasm ("That seminar was so wonderful!") from robbing our good sense. It also provides the stability and continuity our students need.

My greatest help in curriculum choices has always been my husband. It is not because he knows all the ins and outs of the programs I am considering. It is because, when listening is important, he listens. At the beginning of a school year, we often sit down together to make final decisions. I show him the different programs I am considering. I point out the pros and cons. He asks pertinent questions. I explain some more. He tells me what he thinks, and the decisions are made.

Our husbands know us well. After all, they have been studying us for a long time. Because of their slightly removed vantage point, they are also excellent observers of our homeschool. They know when mom is more talk and dreams than action. When various curriculum are explained to them, they will likely know with which ones we are more apt to follow through. They know when we are suiting a program to our interests rather than the needs of the students. They know when we are threatening our students with major overload or when, out of compassion or a desire to avoid confrontation, we are making it too easy on them. Seek your husband's advice. Listen carefully. Then the real challenge begins: will you follow his suggestions?

Taming the Curriculum Changeling

I love children's books. They are often (not always) a vast improvement over adult fiction. Whereas adult fiction often captures one's attention with crudeness and sensationalism, children's books are more apt to do it through cleverness of thought and wordplay. Those who grew up in the forties, fifties, and sixties had some wonderful choices, old and new. Unfortunately adult elements are creeping into books for today's children, but gems are still to be found. Periodically I will read through new Newbery, Caldecott, and Bluebonnet (a Texas honor) award books searching carefully for anything that sparkles. I will also read older books looking for an author I overlooked in my youth.

On one of these searches I read a book about a changeling. Using a plot based on medieval fears and superstitions, it tells of an infant snatched from its cradle by self-serving fairy folk and replaced by a changeling. Although I'm sure in today's horror fiction a changeling would have awful demonic implications, in this book it was basically the story of a colossal brat. (By the way, the story ends happily, with mama and baby reunited and the misfit changeling in a happier living situation.)

Curriculum often has changeling characteristics. We start with something colorful, crisp, and attractive. The fresh printer's ink even smells good! The stack of books looks so neat and inviting. We feel in control. Then one night, generally during the first week of the new school year, something happens. While we sleep, those wonderful, comforting books—the ones destined to make our children geniuses—are snatched away!

We wake up in the morning with an odd sense that something is amiss. We start our school day without mishap, but we soon wear a puzzled frown. "I don't remember this book having so many pages." "I thought this book explained things better than this." "Oh, my goodness, child, give me that book, I didn't know it had *that* in it!" The curriculum changeling has arrived.

Like the child's fairy tale, our story can have a happy ending, but we need to find out how to tame the changeling or carefully send it back home. Unfortunately, it is not unusual for us to invite the changeling into our home. Going to a homeschool convention or bookstore with a light heart and plastic cards or crackling money in your pocket is one way. (The jingling kind doesn't count. You're safe there.) Catalogs spread across your kitchen table and a phone within easy reach has the same effect. We mustn't forget the internet and its easy slide into danger. Changelings can also appear as activities, often suggested by well-meaning homeschool friends, that promise to enhance our schooling immeasurably. At these times we tend to lower our guard. There is no telling what materials will soon be in our home with us or what activities will take us away from the home fires! To avoid unhappy surprises it is vital that you do some advance planning.

Basics and Bonuses

First, start by considering the basics. Do not start with the supplements and the "Oh! That looks fun!" stuff. Methodologies will disagree about the definition of a basic, but primarily the basics are what you really must teach if your children are to be well educated. They are the academic subjects that are important by almost anyone's standards. Skill development books or checklists can sometimes help identify what is basic. The basics will vary according to the age of your child. We will look at them a bit more closely in the next chapter.

Next, decide what extras, or bonuses, you will teach or participate in. These can take two directions. They can be academically based, indepth studies that go beyond the bare minimums. For example, we will all study history, but how we teach it will vary tremendously. One family will read the text and test periodically. Another will read a wide variety of historical fiction and biographies to supplement their text, build models, prepare historical meals, and visit reenactment villages. The latter family is enjoying an academic bonus.

Bonuses can also be extracurricular activities. Music lessons, dance lessons, and athletics fall into this category. Support group activities can be either academic or extracurricular bonuses. Either way, once discovered they can expand the opportunities for enrichment exponentially!

Unlike the basics, the bonuses we choose will vary from family to family. It is not unusual for one family to have a houseful of athletes while another is full of musicians. The academic bonuses and extras we choose celebrate our family's uniqueness. Because I love languages, our homeschool academic bonus is Latin. Our extras include piano and ballet lessons.

Sewing and cooking have joined our extras this year. I remember reading about a family who set up an animation studio in their home—definitely a celebration of their uniqueness!

Academic bonuses and extracurricular activities offer us freedom to both be ourselves and express our special talents. However, they become a bondage when we choose studies and activities because other homeschoolers believe them important. Even when the choices are our own, they can enslave us. There are so many wonderful, worthwhile subjects to study. We can participate in so many marvelous activities. Choose carefully. Overdoing what is good creates a frantic pace that robs your homeschooling of its joy. We all need time for prayer and reflection to choose wisely and appropriately for our family.

To help you in your decision making consider the following ideas. Begin by creating a school plan for the upcoming year. List the areas of study, both basics and bonuses. Under each area enter the books and resources you intend to use. Collect information for those curriculum decisions that remain undecided. Conversations with homeschool moms about their curriculum triumphs and failures can yield valuable information. Careful perusal of catalogs, magazines, website reviews, and curriculum guides, such as those by Cathy Duffy and Mary Pride, offer invaluable second opinions. Retail stores with homeschooling departments, homeschool conventions, and used book sales provide opportunities to closely examine potential choices.

Add all your selections to your school plan. It will often become clear which areas are overloaded with too many good resources. Listing curriculum prices will also add a heavy dose of reality to your plans. Take a deep breath and bravely scratch out those wonderful, but unnecessary, extras. Know that you have saved yourself the guilt of leaving expensive resources idle. You have also saved yourself some dusting.

> *Take a deep breath and bravely scratch out those wonderful, but unnecessary, extras.*

The Place of Creativity

All of us admire the moms of boundless energy who make each day a learning adventure. That has never been me. The myriad responsibilities of my life and the wide span of my children's ages have tended to keep any all-encompassing creativity at low ebb. However, I can be, and often am, selectively creative. I love history. My reading material at bed time is often the latest children's historical fiction (under the guise of reviewing it for the store, you understand). My girls are working on unique accordion fold timelines that display several civilizations at once, folding up when not in use. We have spent many pleasurable hours, mom reading aloud while the girls draw little pictures for their timelines. We work on it most Friday afternoons and it is definitely the highlight of our school week.

So what am I encouraging? Everyone should make accordion fold timelines? No, although we have had a great time with it. What I am encouraging is that you learn to be selectively creative.

We all have areas in which we excel. We all have areas where we feel creative. Whether it involves creating academic bonuses in a beloved subject or planning enticing extracurricular activities, there is something we can do in a special way. However, we don't all have boundless energy.

Therefore, I would encourage you not to think you must reinvent the wheel in every subject. Don't feel you must plan every school subject from scratch. Publishers have spent years developing their scopes and sequences. They put careful thought into their products. Don't be ashamed to tap into their expertise. Don't hang your head if you have chosen to teach history from a textbook instead of through a labor intensive unit study. Don't let creativity run rampant through your home if you don't want time intensive activities to be your constant companions.

Learn to welcome creativity on your terms. *Put your energy and ideas where they will bear the most fruit.* It may be in planning historical unit studies. It may be in producing dramatic plays with costuming. It may be in teaching your girls to quilt or bake. It may be in gardening. It may *not* lie in making colonial samplers to teach the multiplication facts! If you feel your skills are truly nonexistent, your creativity may lie in arranging your schedule and budget so you can get your children to the enriching lessons you desire them to have.

Enjoying Premeditated Flexibility

I am the queen of premeditated flexibility. Spontaneous flexibility is not in my good favor and tends to dwell in the lower realms of my castle.

I have not been one for ditching the schoolwork because the day is pretty. I'm much more given to bribery and incentives: "Oh, such a pretty day! Let's hurry through school so you can go out and enjoy it." As any seasoned homeschooler knows, the same amount of school can take one hour to complete or six, depending on the dispositions and moods of the day. It is possible to get the schoolwork done *and* play outside without being an absolute ogre about it.

Spontaneity rarely flies at our house. Because of this fact, clever children don't pester me: "Oh, look, mom, a beautiful day! Why don't we go outside." (It's overcast and sprinkling.) Except for an occasional cautious inquiry, my children gave up a long time ago.

Over time I have discovered that too much unplanned flexibility gets in the way of quality schooling. Although, for some of us, this is stating the obvious, for others it is a homeschool heresy. Life will always afford us many, many opportunities to shelve the books and follow other pursuits. But I contend that there is a limit to how many trips to the zoo can be considered field trips. Comparison grocery shopping for math class cannot count weekly. Good activities often replace what's best, even if the best is sometimes a bit boring.

In some ways it was easier to homeschool twenty years ago. In those days, the legal status of homeschooling was regularly challenged. Only the most intrepid homeschool moms poked their noses outside their doors before the school buses began their afternoon routes. For eight hours we were tied to our homes with nothing to do but school. It wasn't a bad plan for success.

We can still succeed today without the outside threats of earlier homeschooling days. We can succeed by plodding. Faithful plodding requires planning our schoolwork and then doing what we plan. The little steps each day get the job done. When first time homeschool moms share fears of inadequacy, my question invariably is, "Can you plod? Can you stay with a task to completion?" It is the most important ingredient for success.

But what about flexibility? Do not discard it. Control it. Use it wisely. Change the way you look at it. Consider flexibility as one of the precious blessings of homeschooling. Precious things are not used willy-nilly, but for elevated and worthwhile purposes. Consider some of the following:

• Use flexibility to customize for a child's individual needs. You are not bound to use what others use, even the books your child's sibling used. When possible, use what is best for each child.

• Use flexibility to provide variety in your school program. Use the math text from the company that provides hands-on opportunities for learning. Use the grammar book your child can correct himself. Do your history from read aloud books you choose according to their high interest. Read from quality children's literature, sometimes using accompanying guides. Or use the same company for everything and enjoy the way different subjects often correlate and enhance each other. The choice is yours because of our wonderful flexibility.

• Use your flexibility to skip your schoolwork for worthwhile activities. Kiddie Konzerts at your local fine arts center, support group activities, or visiting the nursing home to sing Christmas carols are all quality options. Make sure you exchange the good for the better.

• Use your flexibility to meet your family's unique scheduling needs. We school two mornings and three afternoons a week. One afternoon a week the girls work independently on assignments I have left them, with dad (who offices at home) available if absolutely necessary. This allows the girls to take smaller morning ballet classes and helps me get my work hours in. Do what works best for your family.

• Use your flexibility to accommodate long range plans. School year round, taking breaks every six or eight weeks. School according to the normal school calendar. It's your choice. Take a week off for a special off-season family vacation. At our home we take much of the month of December off because church obligations multiply.

•Enjoy your flexibility by controlling your flexibility. View it as a precious treasure not to be used flippantly. Be sure activities are worthwhile when detouring from normal school schedules. Road detours at their best are brief, well-marked, and bring us back to our proper path. School detours should share the same characteristics. Finally, give yourself some grace. In a pinch, go ahead and count a trip to Wal-Mart as a field trip—but not too often!

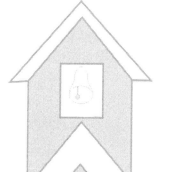

"Begin at the beginning," the King said, very gravely, "and go on till you come to the end: then stop."

The King of Hearts in Alice in Wonderland

Defining the Basics

Sailing with Columbus in a refrigerator box *Santa Maria*. Sampling various apple varieties while wearing a saucepan hat in honor of Johnny Appleseed. Making origami valentine boxes. Eating stew out of bread bowls at a Medieval feast (with our fingers, of course). We have enjoyed all of these delightful activities during our homeschool years. It's the stuff homeschool dreams are made of! It's delightful fun! But is it a daily essential? No. However, it is certainly one of those bonuses we want to enjoy from time to time.

There are daily essentials. They are not always delightful, but we do our best to make them as palatable as possible. They are the basics, and it's time to look at them. Where do we start? I suggest we follow the King of Heart's excellent advice. We will begin at the beginning with preschool and go on till the end with high school, then stop. (We'll leave the college-level homeschooling to another author and another book!)

Over the years I have found myself dividing our school years into five different groupings: preschool, kindergarten through second grade, third through sixth grade, junior high, and high school. Each of the grades within a group share similar challenges and academic goals. Let's look at these five groups and the basics they emphasize.

Preschoolers

Most of us believe we have precocious pre-schoolers. Some of us actually do. Does that mean it is time to start academics?

A number of years ago one of my children served as a guinea pig in our local university's educational program. A graduate student needed to conduct some motor skill testing, and she was assigned my youngest son to evaluate. A week later she invited me to her home to discuss her findings. She was a long time kindergarten teacher very interested in the correlation of motor skill development and academic progress. As we visited, she shared her conviction that the worst thing that ever hit her kindergarten was the administrative direction of favoring academics over motor skill development. She felt it negatively affected her students' long term success in school. I have never forgotten her comments.

Most of us believe we have precocious preschoolers. Some of us actually do.

There are so many fine and wonderful things to do with a preschooler. Educational toys abound, but our littlest ones usually prefer our company. They love to toddle around, sharing in our daily tasks. Folding a washcloth is a satisfying challenge. Cleaning the toilet bowl with that neat brush is indescribable fun (and probably off limits). Helping mom measure ingredients for cookies is a profitable activity, especially if it is accompanied by emptying all the cabinets while Mom cleans up the baking mess. Then it's time to lay down or enjoy a gentle rock while reading the same few books we read before each naptime. They are such good friends and we love them so much! All of this is the genuine preschool adventure. Don't feel the need to rush through it.

Having said that, does that mean I'm against all preschool academics? I'll respond with a cautious no. It does mean I believe readiness skills should not be neglected while academics are rushed. Working on language acquisition, verbal expression, visual discrimination, auditory awareness, and fine and large motor skills should come first. Working on these skills comes quite naturally in the course of a busy toddler's life, especially when accompanied by plenty of parental and sibling interaction.

When it comes to academics, you know your child. You know his capabilities. Most children will let us know when they are frustrated by being pushed too fast and beyond their ability. Read their signals carefully and respond to them immediately. Pushing your preschooler can leave a bad taste for further schooling. It can also steal time (that will never return) from much more precious activities.

Kindergarten through Second Grade

Kindergartners through second graders are in many ways still babies. Your role as a homeschool teacher is an easy and natural extension from motherhood. My little ones have always felt the need for lots of physical contact during school. We often did schoolwork cuddling on the couch. The children learned new math concepts and saw them corrected from the comfort of my lap. If nothing else, they would stand by my chair resting against my side, or put an arm around my shoulder and play with my hair. We call such touchy-feely children *mush monsters* at our house. Enjoy these days!

Fortunately the basics are as simple and natural as the affectionate behavior that goes hand in hand with teaching little ones. I can sum it up in four main points. Anything you add beyond these four points can be considered a nice, nonessential extra:

1. Prepare your child to read.
2. Teach your child to read.
3. Read, read, and read some more.
4. Teach basic math knowledge.

Preparing a child to read involves the readiness skills mentioned in the preschool section above. It means getting them emotionally, verbally, visually, auditorily, and physically ready. Emotionally we equate reading with comfort and pleasure. Time spent snuggling on the couch reading aloud from colorful picture books draws a child towards a lifelong love of reading. Verbally we want to talk about what we read, inviting them to translate their thoughts into words. Visually we share preschool and primary level puzzle books searching each page for what is changed, hidden, or missing. Games, where our young one must decide which item we have removed from a tray, also teach the sharp visual awareness we are striving to develop. Auditorily we listen to tapes at bedtime and play command games, "I want you to touch your nose, turn around, and giggle. Don't start till I'm finished telling you!" We read aloud some more. Physically, we take a deep breath and get out the playdoh that sticks in the carpet, the blunt scissors that find their way into hair, and the glue that appears everywhere.

Teaching our children to read involves choosing a phonics program. Whether you buy the Cadillac or Volkswagon model is between you and your pocketbook. As long as the program is both systematic and thorough it should do its job well. Let the phonics program double as spelling; learn to spell some of those new words you can read. For pleasure reading, progress from the controlled vocabulary readers of your phonics program into *I Can Read* chapter books. The *Henry and Mudge* (Cynthia Rylant) series has been a favorite of ours. The *Frog and Toad* (Arnold Lobel) and *Amelia Bedelia* (Peggy Parrish) series are close seconds.

Decide whether your student will read whole books or use a textbook reading series. Whole books often do the best job of teaching a love of reading. Their length also provides exposure to better developed characterizations and more involved story plots. Depending on our choices, whole book reading can expose our children to either excellent or horrid writing styles. Textbook series often supply us with high level comprehension and critical thinking questions. They also contain a systematic presentation of skills that we may forget to teach without the book's help. Over the course of the school year or from one year to the next, I often move between the two approaches trying to get the best of both worlds.

The majority of your time during these early school years will be spent on reading. The reasons for all that intense effort are simple and direct. Your student is both learning to read and learning to love it. Materials are a vehicle to accomplish these purposes. Their content is not important for permanent recall.

Math is best taught by using a math textbook series and simple manipulatives. Skills in math are taught sequentially. Most of us don't have the background to know, or the time to learn, what is the best order in which to teach skills. Hopping from one curriculum to another can cause significant problems for our students. Although the sequence of skills may be very similar from program to program, the pace at which they introduce those skills can differ drastically. A careless change in program can leave one child repeating what he learned the year before and another child skipping skills that he can't afford to miss.

Math manipulatives are very helpful in teaching abstract math concepts in a concrete manner. A jar of change, rulers, counters, base ten blocks, and Cuisenaire rods have all gotten heavy usage in our home. Invest in a set of base ten blocks. Place-value, borrowing, and carrying should never be a problem again. I have also used Cuisenaire rods or similar products to teach adding, subtracting, skip counting and its correlation with multiplication, and to solve simple equations with an unknown. Idea books can teach you how to use them for many more mathematical concepts.

When reading and math are progressing well, you can add simple science and history books. Some of us may want to add content before the child's independent reading skills are ready. After all, children are capable of understanding much more than they can read for themselves. They can also verbally express much more than they can write down on paper. Reading aloud can again come to our rescue. You can enjoy the many colorful science and history books published for young students. You must determine how much content you want them to permanently retain.

Third Through Sixth Grade

It always happens. Now that you feel warm and cozy about your program and can recite the phonograms in your sleep, you begin to feel a bit of a draft. The winds of change have begun to blow gently, but persistently, through your home. You now have a third grader.

The winds of change have begun to blow gently, but persistently, through your home.

During the third through sixth grades, often called the informational age, students are no longer reading to learn to read. They read to master the information or content that the book contains. At this time some homeschoolers will ease into testing or oral questioning to see how the fact accumulation is going.

Students during these years become more independent in their studies. They still need us frequently, but it gradually lessens as time passes. It's a good thing! The next little blessing may need the majority of mom's attention while learning to read.

At this time basic subjects begin to expand. The always important language art studies begin to change: reading and spelling continue, but phonics slowly disappears. Grammar, punctuation, and composition gradually take its place. Penmanship practice will switch from manuscript to cursive if your program has not already done so. History and science are no longer nice sporadic extras; they are now approaching equal status with language arts and math.

Other subjects may also appear. Latin or other foreign language studies can begin once a child is fluent in reading his own language. You may begin keyboarding, emphasizing correct finger positions before hunt and peck habits become ingrained. Geography, state history, and a little civics may rotate with history. Private music lessons may begin. Art projects, good at any age, will be an enjoyable change of pace.

Students begin looking beyond their own little worlds. Two things have always made me feel that my children were really growing up. One is the loss of the first baby tooth. The other is when they can understand and use the words city, state, and country properly in their casual conversation. To me it's a coming-of-age—the crossing of a threshold from our home and our street to a much bigger world.

The informational age is also a time where school problems may begin to appear. Some children will do fine through second grade but begin a slow slide downwards in third. Often they are still reading to learn to read. Their decoding skills are not yet sharp enough for the comprehension now required. If this is your child, back up and slow down. If you have recently begun homeschooling, it is possible your student did not learn proper word attack skills. He may not know that letters make sounds and words can be sounded out. Perhaps he is aware of this, but his skills are sketchy and incomplete. Or he may be memorizing a word's appearance. Go back and build the phonics foundation now.

Occasionally deeper learning problems cannot be solved by phonics. To be quite honest, our oldest son learned to read quite early and largely by sight. It is not unusual for people with an impairment in one sense to be quite strong in another. However, I did take him through a phonics program, anyway, to fill in gaps and improve his auditory awareness. When we discovered several years later that our next two children shared the same genetic impairment, we chose to continue the systematic phonics program we were using.

If you sense that your student has a learning problem that a strong dose of phonics cannot cure, don't hesitate to seek professional help. Your local homeschool support group should know of qualified individuals in your area who are homeschool friendly. Through the years we have found a number of people who were helpful with our particular situation. They were not averse to training me while training my children in the speech development skills that were necessary.

Seventh and Eighth Grade

Junior high. People teaching these grades are often considered martyrs for a great cause. What makes it difficult?

Our young teens tend to be self-absorbed. Major physical and mental changes are occurring in them. They are beginning the journey of self-discovery that will continue in some measure for the rest of their lives. "Who am I? What do I think about this? What do they think about me? What do I believe? Am I pretty? Am I ugly? Why am I so incredibly stupid?" What a hard age!

While they explore their thoughts and values, they will sometimes distance themselves from ours. This may hurt our feelings. We may choose to see it as rebellion. (Undoubtedly, some of it is.) Alternatively, we can choose to see it as the process of our children maturing into individuals, of weaning themselves off our thoughts and determining their own. Dorothy Sayers, an early proponent for a return to a classical philosophy of education, called it the pert stage—a gentle phrase for "argumentative." What opportunities these times are for parental prayer!

Into this maelstrom of thoughts and emotions we try to throw some academics. The good news is, although some may disagree with me, I don't see this as a time to teach many new concepts. A major change occurs in textbooks, however. Print size, which took a dive around third or fourth grade, will take another dive now. This tremendously expands the content contained in each book. At this point weaker students may again struggle. Strong reading skills become more vital than ever.

Into this maelstrom of thoughts and emotions we try to throw some academics.

Basics will change slightly but retain a connection to earlier studies. Reading will grow into literature. Literature will introduce some well-established works that students will study for literary elements and read for comprehension. Spelling takes a back seat to vocabulary acquisition, but should be continued concurrently if the student is not a good speller. If you haven't already used a systematic grammar study, you will probably begin now. Penmanship continues only when a student needs it. Composition will teach proper sentence structure, paragraph formation, and multiple paragraph essays. For some students, the five paragraph essay may culminate in a short research paper using a few sources.

Junior high math will brush up mathematical skills and begin pre-algebra. Bright math students may begin algebra in eighth grade. Weaker students have a little more time to cement their skills before tackling it.

History and science will contain much more content; most was introduced in an abbreviated form in earlier grades. This provides our students with memory hooks for attaching more data. History surveys American and world history. Alternatively, government or state history may be studied. Science may offer earth, life, or general science which serve as introductions to future high school coursework.

Additional courses may be studied or introduced. In order to help mom by printing out compositions, students may learn basic word processing. A jumpstart on high school foreign languages can also be helpful.

High School

Bringing three children through high school, writing a book on it, and navigating college admissions for the third time, I don't find it a particularly threatening process. Hard work, yes. Tedious at times, yes. But not scary. I know it can be. Take heart! It can be done!

High school is primarily a preparation for the future. I believe it is advantageous for every intellectually capable student to prepare for college. We have no crystal ball that foretells a child's path or future circumstances. The better prepared he is for any eventuality, the more confidence we can have in his future.

On occasion I have heard customers express their family's conviction that they ought not prepare their daughters for college but should focus on homemaking skills and preparation to be a wife and mother. I am always troubled when I hear this. Like most homeschool mothers, it is my first desire for my girls to be wives and mothers. I do my best to train them in lifeskills and godly character accordingly. However, I also want them to have sharp, biblically-trained minds and a well developed Christian worldview. I want them to be equipped to counsel their children wisely in their encounters with the many different issues of life. This goal is both compatible with and necessary for effective motherhood and the schooling of their own children. I also desire for them to have the education and skills to become bread winners, should it ever prove necessary.

I know that life is unpredictable and, through God's sovereignty, takes twists and turns we would never have expected or chosen. Many girls will discover that a single life is God's will for them and will need skills to support themselves. Many wives will unexpectedly find themselves thrust into the workforce due to a husband's disability or death. Sometimes a husband's income will need to be supplemented temporarily to cover unbudgeted needs, not wants, that arise. By not preparing for life's unexpected but all too common occurrences we potentially condemn our daughters and possibly their children to a minimum wage, poverty level lifestyle.

Having said that, I would recommend encouraging our girls to enter fields that are compatible with motherhood. Education degrees prepare them for the classroom, substituting, tutoring, or capably teaching their own children. Music degrees prepare them for taking private students, holding a pianist position in the church, and enriching their family with beauty. Accounting makes way for them to keep the books for a small business or a family business of their own. Nursing can be a helpful skill for any mother and is seldom a saturated field. These career fields can either be pursued from home or offer very flexible scheduling. This list is just a start; undoubtedly there are many possibilities I have missed.

Should you agree with my reasoning and believe that college preparation is wise, the first step is to plan a high school program that can accomplish this goal. What are the high school basics? What is required for a student to be accepted into college?

One safe way to choose your high school program is to send for a catalog and an application packet from the college (or colleges) your student is considering. The catalog will usually contain a list of preferred high school courses for applicants. If it is not in the catalog, contact the admissions department for the needed information. Then plan your coursework accordingly.

Getting college entrance information early in your high school process will save you anxiety, money, and unhappy surprises. Knowing what the college expects can help you plan your program in an orderly sequence, saving you from rushing around senior year to fill gaps and reducing the anxiety that surrounds an already stressful process.

Regarding money, the more you know about a college's scholarship opportunities and evaluation process, the more likely you will find a scholarship program to your student's advantage. Our third child will most likely attend college out of state next year. Although we are working on a normal college admission's schedule, had we sought out earlier scholarship information we might have been able to change some last minute strategies resulting in an education cost savings of several thousand dollars a year. We are still learning!

To prevent most last minute, unhappy surprises get your facts early. Recently I heard that one of our more competitive state universities added a third year of foreign language to its high school requirements. That is not something you want to find out in your student's senior year!

The whole process of planning a high school program is a lengthy one, with courses to choose and plan, a transcript to assemble, and a GPA to calculate. Other items a college sometimes requests such as course descriptions and portfolios of student work cannot be produced successfully at the last minute. For information on these high school topics and many others, I refer you to my book, *Home-Designed High School*. I believe you will find that I have presented the information in as painless and thorough a manner as possible. (See blatant self-promotion at end of book)

And let the beauty of the LORD our God be upon us, and establish the work of our hands for us; yes, establish the work of our hands. (Psalm 90:17)

And I will pray the Father, and He will give you another Helper, that He may abide with you forever, even the Spirit of truth, whom the world cannot receive, because it neither sees Him nor knows Him; but you know Him, for He dwells with you and will be in you. (John 14:16,17)

Come to Me, all you who labor and are heavy laden, and I will give you rest. Take My yoke upon you and learn from Me, for I am gentle and lowly in heart, and you will find rest for your souls. For My yoke is easy and My burden is light. (Matthew 11:28-30)

Controlling Our Commitments

My husband and I have lived in the same community for twenty-two years. He has pastored the same church for twenty. Yet what appear to be very stable circumstances have resulted in a ceaseless parade of changes which often amazes us. Life is never static!

A major change occurred this year on the home front. Our oldest daughter, with our sincere blessing, left the nest to migrate a mere 900 miles from home. When friends asked her how her mother felt about her move, she was quick to tell them I had done the same thing in my enthusiastic youth. What we do to our parents returns to haunt us!

Tears of good bye were mixed with happy anticipation for my younger daughters. They would have their own bedrooms now! Then a chain of unhappy events began for our overanxious girls, something similar to Christmas being unexpectedly delayed a month. A plumbing flood destroyed the carpet in one of the rooms. We repaired the plumbing and ordered new carpet. Two weeks passed. A call to inquire about the delay revealed that the carpet was on backorder. More time passed. Our next call found us offering condolences to the installer who had broken his collarbone. We called again, hopefully allowing a polite passage of time for convalescence. The carpet company was so sorry, they said, but the pattern had been discontinued. Could we choose another?

We ordered new carpet, due to arrive the first of the week. At that point my husband suggested I get away for a few days to work on this manuscript. I had a deadline I needed to meet and I was getting nowhere fast. With the long anticipated carpet coming and bedrooms to set up it would be hard to get much schoolwork done. I could leave the girls some independent schoolwork. Dad would keep the home fires lit and muscle the furniture into place.

I considered the idea. A visiting pastor was filling the pulpit Sunday; my husband's work load was lighter than usual. I knew I would have no problem getting the time off work. The girls would be settling into their new rooms savoring each moment. Even though I would have a mountain of corrections to do when I returned, a reasonable amount of school could still be accomplished. Life could be successfully rearranged. The idea was providential!

When I left, I felt badly that my youngest daughter cried. "What will happen to the book we are reading at bedtime?" she wailed. "We only have three chapters left!" From past experience she knew it was dangerous to take an unexpected break from a book. We had begun a book about a camping adventure one summer and then put it up for a few days. The poor characters were left in their flimsy tents to freeze through the winter. We rescued them the following spring. Now we were reading about the same children on another grand summer campout. We couldn't do the same thing to them again! With some difficulty I convinced her we would be more faithful this time.

My daughter's concerns were bred from years of living in our household. She was well aware of how often the urgent received an undue portion of her parent's time. So many things clamor for our attention, in both the activities of our life and homeschooling.

The Pushmi-pullyu of Homschooling

When I was young I read through the entire Dr. Dolittle series by Hugh Lofting. I loved the books. One of his characters was an odd creature called a pushmi-pullyu. It was a llama-like creature, with a head at each end. The pushmi-pullyu was a gentle, shy creature who had worked out the unique challenges of his anatomy well.

It is a good thing I was not created a pushmi-pullyu.

For example, one mouth did all the talking, the other all the eating. It was a satisfactory arrangement, agreeable to both ends of the beast.

It is a good thing I was not created a pushmi-pullyu. I would have been quite dysfunctional. I'm sure I would have wanted to debate who ate each meal, which direction we would stroll afterwards, and who would get stuck walking backwards. The resulting confusion and chaos would probably bear a striking resemblance to my life.

For years I have lived a too busy lifestyle, often attempting to go in two directions at once. Mother, pastor's wife, homeschool teacher, part-time employee, writer, housewife, cook—all roles which truly bring me delight. But playing all the roles simultaneously is heart stopping. Your combination of roles may be significantly different from mine, but I imagine its heart stopping capabilities are just as real. How do we meet the challenge? How do we juggle it all? How do we keep some sense of calm and well-being?

It certainly helps not to be a perfectionist. Unfortunately, I succumbed to this state of existence years ago. Perhaps you have, too. As perfectionists, we not only do it all but expect to do it all well. We live in a constant state of motion. We seesaw between adrenaline charged activity and collapse. I read Matthew 11:28-30 and want to cry out, "The burden is not easy! The yoke is not light! Help me!"

There are certainly spiritual answers to my questions, but there are practical considerations, too. I will start with the pragmatic, and save the heart-to-heart for last.

The Myth of Excellence

Last year I found some help for my perpetual state of frantic activity from an unexpected and unlikely source. I was reading a business book the store manager thought I would enjoy. It had some ideas he believed would be useful for the bookstore. He encouraged several of his employees to read it and looked forward to discussing it with us.

The title of the book is *The Myth of Excellence* (Fred Crawford and Ryan Mathews, Crown Publishing, 2001). The title alone is enticing for an overloaded perfectionist! Supported by a wealth of examples, it is an intriguing read for the business owner who is rethinking his marketing strategies. However, the surprise came when I realized its underlying principles could be profitably applied to other areas of life, including homeschooling.

The premise of the book is that no store can do everything well. Each store has to *choose* the areas in which it will excel. It has to *choose* what will set it apart from its competition.

The book lists five important areas of competition. Business owners are urged to evaluate their performance by prioritizing each area, descending from their greatest strength.

These five areas are then assigned a value. The most important area ranks a five, the next a four. The rest are ranked at three. There are no ones or twos. The most important area, the five, represents an area where the business truly excels. It is what they are known for, what established their reputation with their customers. It is what sets them apart from their competition. The number four area is an area of great strength. It is done extremely well. However, it doesn't have all the bells and whistles and perfections of area five. Then come the threes. Threes are areas that are adequate. They do not set you apart. They are not unique. They don't call attention to themselves, but they certainly get an acceptable job done. The ones and twos are the no-nos. They are the gas station restroom without a door in the *Geech* cartoon strip. They are unacceptable, undesirable, and a customer will not put up with them.

Now to the point. In our homeschools we need to make some choices. We need to choose the subject or subjects (no more than a couple, please) that will be our fives. We have to choose our fours. We will have to be satisfied to have threes, not seeing them as unsightly blemishes on our homeschool character.

We *cannot* be excellent in everything! It is not a good choice to expend all of our energy struggling to achieve perfection in our homeschooling. The result will be exhausted mediocrity, or worse, in other important areas of life. Our relationship with the Lord and our husbands, church activities, friendships, and homemaking skills should not all be pitiful ones and twos hidden in a bulging closet.

We cannot be excellent in everything!

We will all make our rankings differently. Your five star subject will be different than mine. What I declare a three, you may elevate to a five. Our personal strengths and weaknesses and our children's future goals will help determine each placement. We can make our determinations with I Corinthians 12 again in mind, realizing that we, children included, will not be at our peak performance as an eye if God intended us to be an excellent ear.

There are benefits to this approach. We can get rid of feelings of guilt and discard unnecessary activities. It can provide time and energy for other things. We might even be able to dust off a few ones or twos and move them to a more respectable position.

Broadening the Application

When I had only two or three children, I used to wash my kitchen floor on my hands and knees. I wanted every crack and crevice clean. I wanted the Cheerios my toddler discarded on the floor to be safe for consumption when he inevitably returned for them.

A few years ago I saw a friend at the funeral of a mutual acquaintance. We hadn't seen each other in years. I expected her to ask about my older children, whom she had once known well. She didn't. To my surprise she queried, "Do you still wash your kitchen floor on your hands and knees?" I smiled and commented that life was too busy for that anymore. If I had been more honest, I might have responded, "You're supposed to clean kitchen floors? I thought that was the dog's job!"

There are many activities in life, not just washing kitchen floors, that we wish to give our best efforts. It simply can't be done. When I began work at the bookstore, it required a major reworking of my priorities. There are many things I no longer do. Although my job provides a good bit of flexibility, I try not to use it. Those hours will have to be made up at a less convenient time requiring me to give mediocrity to an area I desire to give excellence.

I like to schedule my life. I like a predictable order. I find it helps me get more accomplished. I know where I am going and what I am doing each day. I don't rely on my memory; it is all committed to paper. The schedule tends to change each January, June, and September. For a while I will rely on my paper, but before long I have trained myself like Pavlov's dogs. Then I refer to my schedule only when life has been out of sync or I am brain dead from the weekend.

Let me encourage you to examine how you are spending your time. What areas consume more time than they are worth? Are you putting the effort for a five star activity into something that merits three star attention?

Over the passage of time I have learned to drop some of my perfectionistic tendencies. It has not come easily. At times I have taken a rebellious stance, "If I can't do it right, I won't do it at all!" This rebel cry has often led me to drop some standards too low. Instead of becoming satisfactory threes, they became blatant ones. Hence, the sad state of my kitchen floor. I tell myself when life slows down I will return to my earlier habits of excellence. I doubt it. It will not happen for several reasons. First of all, washing my floor on my hands and knees is a waste of good time. Hopefully, I'll have grandchildren I could be playing with. Secondly, my knees and hips grumble and groan when I get off the floor now.

What makes me think it will be easier later? Most importantly, I hope I will have grown in wisdom. I hope I will be like Mary in the book of Luke, who did not fret and flutter about, but chose the better part and sat at Jesus' feet.

Heart-to-Heart Time

Now for the heart-to-heart. Proper homeschool etiquette demands that I invite you for a steaming cup of hot herb tea. I should also add a plate of warm, homemade cookies served on fine china plates with lace napkins. It's the homeschool thing to do!

Unfortunately, I am not at home, where *undoubtedly* I could meet every refined expectation. I will have to leave you to your own devices. Actually, if you can produce tea and a plate of homemade cookies at a moment's notice, you have my deepest admiration. At the moment, the best I can do is a buttered graham cracker. I can't even produce a paper napkin, let alone a lace one. I forgot to bring any with me. I could offer toilet paper, but it really wouldn't hold up for the purpose very well, would it? Besides, it's lacking a bit in dignity.

However, the tea is easier. I love tea, so I'll happily drink it while we chat. The hard part is the *steaming* part. My tea is invariably lukewarm. That's because life always gets in the way. It's steaming when I set it on the table. Actually, steaming a bit too much, so I go on to other projects. I always intend to return at just the right moment. I finally do return, and I take a sip. My tea is cold. Not cold enough to be refreshing, just cold enough to be insipid. Once again I've missed the magic moment for tea drinking perfection. In over 40 years of dedicated tea drinking I have yet to get it right.

While you sip perfectly-temperatured tea and eat your warm cookie, I'll lick the butter off my fingers and take a tepid sip. Let's see what comfort and advice the Lord has for us.

The Beauty of the LORD

Psalm 90:17 has become a regular prayer of mine in the last several years. The psalmist prays that the beauty of the LORD our God would rest upon *us*. (It's nice he included others in his prayer.) Many different names of God could have been used in this psalm. For example, he could have used Adonai, the name of God referring to His power. Instead he uses Yahweh, God's personal name—the name that stresses His covenant making, relationship building nature, the name that stresses God's love for man. It is this beauty, the joy of living in close relation to a God who loves him, that the psalmist most desires in his own life and in ours.

There is no task of higher eternal value than shepherding the lambs God has given us.

After asking for God's beauty to rest upon us, the psalmist then asks God to establish the work of our hands. I don't think the psalmist is speaking only of tasks of everyday living. I believe he is asking Yahweh, the covenant making God, to bless his tasks of eternal consequence. There is no task of higher eternal value than shepherding the lambs God has given us. This is where we most desire the work of our hands to be established and the beauty of the Lord to rest.

Twenty-four Hours a Day

An author I once read recommended making a list of all the things we felt we *had* to do in a day, then estimating how much time each activity would take. Some people took his suggestion. They found they needed *more* than twenty-four hours a day to accomplish everything they felt they absolutely must do. He then delivered his profound question. If the Savior was given only twenty-four hours a day to accomplish a task of incomparable magnitude, why should we need more?

Scripture does not indicate that the tightness of the deadline in any way flustered the Savior. He set about His tasks faithfully. He spent hours in intimate fellowship with His Father. He enjoyed weddings. He ate meals with friends. He shared deep discussions with His disciples. He spoke compassionately with those spurned by society. He sorrowed and wept and comforted bereaved friends. He enjoyed children. His focus was His Father and the sheep His Father had given Him. He pursued the fellowship of His Father and a richness in human relationships.

Our Helper

As the earthly ministry of Jesus drew to a close, He sought to comfort His disciples. Although they did not fully comprehend the awful truth of His impending death, they did understand that He was leaving. In this context of sorrow He offers the comfort they need. Jesus tells them in John 14:16,17 that the Father will send a helper. This helper will abide with them forever. He will be an indwelling reminder of Christ's continuing love for them. He will not leave them alone.

We also are Christ's disciples if we humbly recognize Him as our Savior and King. We share in the blessings of the indwelling Spirit. He will be our helper. He will dwell in us in intimate relationship. We, too, will not be left alone.

The Fullness of God in Relationship with Man

What a wonder! The fullness of God is bound to fallen man. His blessed purpose is to dwell in us: be one with us. His thoughts toward His redeemed are precious and vast beyond counting. He has given relationship with man infinite worth at a cost on Calvary beyond our comprehending.

How differently we live our lives. So often relationships are sacrificed to the activity which consumes us. We neglect our time alone with God to take care of a pressing demand. We neglect the corporate worship of God because we are exhausted from overextending ourselves during the week. Our children speak to us and we grunt a response, never looking up from the task at hand. Our husbands make a statement. We murmur a nondescript answer and continue our supper preparations. Often we do not even look at the person who has sought our attention. We forget to value the beauty of relationship.

Let us change our ways. Let us look at God's incomparable example, with which He so richly blesses us. May we walk through this life with a renewed purpose, stressing relationships, not activities. May we develop a growing calmness in spirit, bestowing our love and attention where it is due instead of on activities that tyrannize our time. May we learn to love our Savior well and the people that are such a blessing in our lives. Then we will find the yoke easy and the burden light.

It sounds good, doesn't it? But how do we do it? Not easily, I'm sure. Activities and things have silent voices that can scream very loudly at us. "We want attention! This really must be done! You can't leave this off your schedule!"

So many of the choices before us are good ones. A change may involve exchanging the good for the better, the better for the best. It may mean analyzing activities and prioritizing their importance. What rating does an activity deserve? Is it absolutely necessary? Is it just a good idea? Should I do it only if there's time? Am I only doing it to meet expectations? The decision making process and final choices will be different for each of us.

Even after some serious consideration, we will often find that the plate is still too full. In the next chapter we will talk about the use of scheduling to help us carry our daily loads with a lighter step.

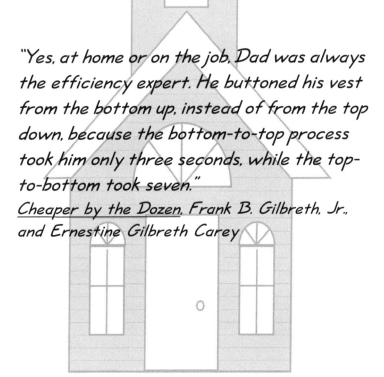

"Yes, at home or on the job, Dad was always the efficiency expert. He buttoned his vest from the bottom up, instead of from the top down, because the bottom-to-top process took him only three seconds, while the top-to-bottom took seven."
Cheaper by the Dozen, Frank B. Gilbreth, Jr., and Ernestine Gilbreth Carey

Scheduling

Cheaper by the Dozen is the true story of the Gilbreth family. With a large family of twelve children, Mr. Gilbreth regularly put his occupational talents to use in his home life. As an efficiency expert, he required each child capable of writing to initial work and progress charts daily. These charts kept track of everything from teethbrushing to homework completion.

As a child, I watched a film version of the book. If I recall correctly, Father always carried a stopwatch in his waistcoat pocket, making every mundane daily task a "motion study." I found it fascinating. Perhaps this explains my motivated search for the least busy route to each of my most common destinations, while mindful of the traffic load at various times of day. It may also explain my continuing interest in lists and charts.

Lifeskill Checklists

I have made it a goal over the last twenty years to design ways of streamlining the mundane processes of life, with homeschooling being a significant focus of my attentions. I have arrived at one simple but profound truism. It is undoubtedly my greatest contribution to the homeschool efficiency study: "If I'm talking too much, I am not organized enough."

I really do get tired of hearing myself talk. It's such hard work! I have a profound respect for silence. I admire the energy and vivacity of people who can fill each silence they encounter, yet it makes my head spin and makes me want to crawl into bed from exhaustion.

With a touch of nostalgia for Mr. Gilbreth's methodologies and a desire to protect my feeble constitution from voice pollution, I have usually operated my homeschool with some variation of a checklist. It helps both life and school run more smoothly.

I have usually operated my homeschool with some variation of a checklist.

It keeps me from inflicting my children with constant questions. We are all happier and accomplish more.

When my oldest children were young, we kept very thorough *lifeskills* checklists. I didn't want to ask whether they had made their bed, brushed their teeth, or fed the dog before school started each day. I wanted those little checks on the list to tell me silently instead. It worked quite well. It recorded tasks which my memory would have failed to recall. I was talking less, they were getting their chores done, school was generally starting on time, and we were all happier. Although I hesitate to report it, in the interest of veracity I imagine I must. The checklists did not have the happy result of turning my grown children into neatniks.

Academic Checklists

For many years I kept academic records in spiral notebooks. They provided more room than a teacher's plan book for keeping notes. But over the years I lost some zeal. I was getting writer's cramp. I didn't want to keep so many notes. It was then I made my second profound observation, "If I'm writing too much, I am not organized enough."

It was then that I developed academic checklists. There are many fine teacher plan books on the market, but I disliked having to write the subject name in each little box. Just think of all the energy and seconds wasted! The tables function of our word processing program put an awesome tool in my hands. I began designing assignment sheets customized for our homeschool, with each box labeled with subject names, subject boxes listed in our normal school day order, space for writing the day's assignments, and smaller boxes for students to check off completed schoolwork.

I was talking less and writing less. Now it was time to figure out ways to get the information into the students' heads more efficiently. This quest led to my third profound observation, "If it can be done in five or ten minutes each day, it will stick better than thirty minutes once a week." Thus began my search for daily academic vitamins.

Academic Vitamins

In our more recent years of homeschooling we have utilized short daily drills in a number of areas. These areas change according to the needs at the time. The drilled areas have included: Bible verses, catechism, math facts (such as timed fact sheets, flashcards, or Learning Wrap-ups), word problems, grammar, English mechanics, reading comprehension, poetry memorization, map skills, geography facts, and Latin declensions and conjugations. The drills are done in the same order every day. The girls know the routine and zip through quickly. Anything needing checking I correct immediately and the girls make needed changes. Each completed book is placed upside down on the cabinet, with the first book completed on the bottom of the stack.

We then move on to our more time consuming subjects, adding each completed book to our upside down stack. When the last book is finished, I flip over each girl's stack and we're ready for tomorrow. How's that for efficiency? Mr. Gilbreth would have been proud of me!

(This method can be hazardous if you first complete a small format catechism book or math flashcards. Placed upside down on the bottom of the stack they will topple everything in short measure. From experience I quickly learned I *had* to set small items to the side.)

Bonus Time

Despite all the previous discussion, I am not obsessed with checklists and a consistent daily order. I am driven by the time I can save to spend in more pleasurable ways. I want time for reading aloud. I want time for my girls to go to ballet, practice piano, and read quality books silently. I want time for them to sew and do the crafts they enjoy. I want time for them to learn cooking skills. I want them to jump on the trampoline. I want them to play with the dogs. All of these bonuses don't happen every day, but, without the time saving efforts we make, they would happen much less often than they do.

A second thing drives me. Having graduated three students and dealt with college entrance testing and academic scholarships, I am aware of how much I need my students to learn and how little time I have. I am aware of my weak areas with my older children. I want my younger students to be able to attend the college of their choice. I want them to be prepared to pursue any scholarships that are available for them. I want to accomplish this without academics consuming us. Therefore, we must be efficient in our studying.

I have learned a few other things about scheduling and efficiency in our time spent homeschooling. Let me share a potpourri of ideas on the topic. I may also throw a few other peripheral thoughts into the pot while I'm stirring it.

An Efficiency Potpourri

• A predictable order is not onerous. It is onerous to have a teacher who is unpredictable. The children never know if the school day will be a breeze or a meeting with Attila the Hun. Little children love predictability and routine; that's why they ask you to read the same book each evening for six months running. Older children want to know your expectations. Don't disappoint them.

•Having a predictable order is not the opposite of creativity and flexibility. It enhances the ability to be creative and flexible. Recently we enjoyed the fruit of this principle. We were having a really beautiful fall day and a cold front was due in the next morning. Our oldest son wanted to take our younger daughters to the zoo to celebrate the beautiful weather. I felt quite comfortable saying yes because our school week had been quite productive. I had no regrets or guilt. It was a great memory-building time for my son and the girls.

•Stay with your young children during schooltime. Even some teens will need this attention. Sit at the table with them. Sometimes we expect too much from our students. We cannot expect them to stay on task if we aren't there to guide them. Be there for questions, efficient corrections, moral support, and, of course, for mid-morning snack time!

•Have a permanent place for each child's schoolwork. We use shelves in a cabinet for books and a cleaning carryall for school supplies. A box or milk crate moved from location to location counts as a permanent place, too, and allows the school location to change.

•Organize loose papers. We have always used color coded spiral notebooks. Each child has his own color. I write the child's name and the subject in permanent marker on the front cover. This means we can look at and discuss error patterns on the last six spelling tests (or do other equally exciting activities) without a frantic search for lost papers.

•Make corrections as soon as work is completed if at all possible. Schoolwork is best learned by association to facts already known. New information is hooked to old information already stored in the brain. Information that has no hook to hang on may be quickly forgotten. Conversely, once information is hooked, it is not as easily forgotten. To keep this process efficient and accurate, make corrections as soon as possible. Give the students accurate hooks to hang new information on. *It is much more efficient to take the extra time to learn it correctly initially than to try to undo all the associations the brain has made with inaccurate information.*

•As discussed previously, learn your rote schoolwork efficiently. This provides more time for critical thinking. Rote versus critical thinking is often debated in homeschool circles. Actually, both are necessary. Rote drill will get those math facts and states and capitals memorized. Critical thinking is vital for a Christian to be able to navigate the social morass in which we live. To oversimplify the matter, rote memory helps us with the black and whites of life; critical thinking helps us understand and evaluate the grays.

• Every battle is not important. Don't waste your time fighting each one. I have chosen to surrender in the battle over proper pencil holds. I fought the battle for years with my oldest daughter. She is self-supporting now and holds a responsible job. I don't believe a correct pencil hold was a criteria for her hiring. When my youngest had a natural affinity to the same incorrect hold, I chose to largely ignore it. She uses a pencil grip that requires the proper pencil hold when practicing penmanship. In other schoolwork I leave her alone. I don't know irrefutably that this was the right decision. I just felt my efforts were better spent in other areas. We all need wisdom to know which battles to expend our energies on and which aren't worth fighting.

• Short but true, the most efficient and best curriculum (if you can say there is a best) is what actually gets done.

• Don't be too much of a homeschool idealist. Life will get in the way. The rule in the retail world is to underpromise and overdeliver. That makes everyone happy. If we can adopt a similar philosophy in homeschooling, we will set reasonable goals and be quite pleased with ourselves when we surpass them.

• Misplaced guilt is very inefficient. The time we spend worrying about what we haven't accomplished could be spent accomplishing something.

•Being humble is efficient. Sometimes when I am stocking books I can't help overhearing conversations. I have noticed a tenuous pattern. Brand new homeschoolers are nervous and unsure of themselves. *Occasionally* homeschoolers of three to five years consider themselves quite knowledgeable and are good for some lengthy advice. Homeschoolers begin to drop in wisdom around year seven and are positively ignorant by year twenty. If you watch your flow of knowledge in years three through five, you can save yourself considerable time not having to eat your words later.

•Look for homemaking areas that can be streamlined. We began following a six week menu plan this year. Each child cooks and cleans up one evening meal each week (the menu was chosen with their abilities in mind). Master grocery lists were developed for each week's meals. Before I head to the store I cross out what I already have and check sale circulars for anything I'll need in the next couple weeks. Shopping has become much easier and we spend far fewer fast food dollars. (Note: A three to four week plan includes enough variety to work well, too. In typical perfectionistic style, I took a good idea and doubled it!)

•Efficiency is not everything. I have often thought it would be convenient if we could run children through mazes like laboratory rats. The outcome of the experiments would help us know which path through the maze of life was best for them. We would know what choices would lead to their success. How efficient! Thankfully, our children are not rats. We don't have to rely on mazes to aid us in our decision making as we prepare them for the future. We have something infinitely better. We have the love and guidance of their Heavenly Father.

For I delight in the law of God according
to the inward man. But I see another law
in my members, warring against the law
of my mind, and bringing me into captivity
to the law of sin which is in my members.
O wretched man that I am! Who will deliver me from this body of death? I thank
God—through Jesus Christ our Lord!
(Romans 7:22-25a)

In the world you will have tribulation; but
be of good cheer, I have overcome the
world. (John 16:33b)

Dealing with Difficult Children

A couple of years ago I attended a seminar at a homeschool convention that was of special interest to me. I had heard the mother speak years before and had been impressed. She had a gentle, godly spirit firmly tethered to earth by her practical nature. I liked the combination.

The seminar was different than I expected. With her daughter's presence and support, she shared a long standing rift between them that the Lord in His mercy had healed. I was deeply touched by their humility and obvious desire to give God the glory. They blessed me and, I am sure, a great many others that day.

I greatly admired this family's courage, but also felt a little uneasy and protective. Homeschoolers, like any other sinful human group, have been known to shoot their wounded. This family, in their desire to bless, was giving a large group of people an unobstructed target. Some sinner in the audience might take aim. I am sure they recognized that possibility but followed God's leading anyway.

Homeschool Humility

Let's face it; sometimes we homeschoolers can be a bit self-righteous. We tout our particular brand of homeschooling and can be a trifle offended when others don't dash to embrace our ideas. Often we can't say the words *public school* without a touch of superiority in our voice. At times we even view private school friends with some suspicion. The homeschool rumor mill can be very active indeed, especially if there is a black sheep in the fold.

God bless you if the previous paragraph left you with no twinges of guilt. You are honoring God in a way many of us have failed. May we all grow daily in humility! However, before we all get too harsh on ourselves or turn maudlin, it doesn't hurt to see how we got this way.

For years we fought battles to establish homeschooling as a creditable educational alternative. In courtrooms, statehouses, magazines and newspapers, public school administration buildings, Grandma and Grandpa's living room, and over the back fence we hammered home our claims and rejoiced when studies proved what we already knew to be true. We became experts at positive public relations. Then a miracle happened. People slowly began to believe us. They began to leave us alone. Inch by inch, we won.

We became experts at positive public relations.

The battle continues but not with the intensity of the early years. We can actually remove our armor as long as we keep it close. Perhaps it is also time to stop embracing our public relations message so heartily. I recommend no changes on the public front; there we must keep the message of homeschool achievement loud and clear. However, when we see that the larger reality of national homeschool achievement doesn't always translate into daily success at home, we should find ourselves growing in humility and mercy.

Merciless pride can harm our comrades-in-arms. It is natural for us to swell with pride over the abilities of our children. It is even more natural for homeschool moms, who devote what feels like every waking moment to the lives of their children, to want to bask in the warmth of a job well-done, but be sensitive. Everyone is not riding high. Many are wounded and tired.

Difficult Children? In the Homeschool Community? Can It be True?

Yes, it can be true, and it is. I'm not talking about the family that never grasped the concept of godly discipline and let their kids run wild. I am talking about difficult children in families where Christian obedience is taken very seriously and mom and dad labor daily to raise their children in the nurture and admonition of the Lord. Perhaps I am talking about your family. I know I am talking about mine. We try very hard to raise our children properly, but the lessons don't always stick with the intensity of crazy glue.

When our children are young, their disobediences are of a minor nature with minor consequences. We know our five year old daughter has not ruined her opportunities for success in life because she has lied to us. However, we do know that persistent small offenses sometimes represent character weaknesses that can create lifelong struggles, even though situations and specifics will change. When our children are young we also find that the force of our will can suppress most difficult outward behavior. The need for our approval is a powerful force in their lives. So much of their world revolves around parents and family. However, even young ones can be quite hard headed in their rebellion. We can admonish and instruct them, gently encouraging a heart change. Despite our valiant efforts, we cannot force their sinful hearts to repent. It is the work of the Holy Spirit to soften the heart.

As our children get older it becomes harder to impose outward obedience. Inward obedience remains the province of God. Our teens are thinking thoughts they do not always share with us. Classes, activities, and part-time jobs thrust them into the world without our presence. We cannot be with them every waking hour, nor should we be. The enticing temptations of the world may be laid at their feet. There may be subtle hints that all is not well. There may be glaring evidences. We may be shocked into awareness by a sudden crisis.

As faithful, loving parents we do not shirk the battle but do our best to confront sin every time it rears its ugly head. In moments of weakness when the battle rages and our energies are low, we may ask ourselves a bewildered question. *Why this battle? We homeschool to avoid all this.* We search for answers. We feel an array of uncomfortable emotions. We are disappointed in our children's choices. We may be bitter towards our hard working spouse, believing had he been more present we might have avoided the problem. Even when the struggle is private we may feel embarrassment before other homeschoolers. *If they only knew how our family struggles, they wouldn't be so friendly to me.*

Hardest of all, we can feel like *personal* failures despite all our faithful efforts. After all, we think, really dedicated homeschoolers don't have these problems. *Perhaps I didn't read the right parenting books. Perhaps I didn't say the right words. Perhaps I was not wise enough in my discipline. Perhaps I expected too much. Perhaps I've been too much of a pushover.* Perhaps we can perhaps ourselves to death!

The first homeschooling students have begun to grow up. We read the success stories in the homeschool magazines and books. For the most part we are proud of what we see. But many homeschoolers whisper that the journey wasn't as easy as they had hoped.

I know many, many homeschoolers. I talk with them weekly in the bookstore. Sometimes I meet them for the first time as they share a troubling situation. Sometimes they are friends I hold very dear. I have cried with some of them. They have cried with me. We have discovered that homeschooling did not protect our children from every evil tendency known to man.

Sometimes easy solutions exist. The heart lifts. Tears dry quickly. Children repent. Sometimes the pain is of a deeper nature with ongoing struggles that make the heart sick while we wait on God's providence for a resolution. Why, after all the sacrifice and ceaseless attempts to encourage godliness do some children struggle so?

I believe there are two basic reasons, one practical and one theological.

The Uncle Billy Effect

Practically, I believe that genetics affects more than just our physical attributes. I believe it plays a strong role in our personalities. People really can get Uncle Billy's temper along with his red hair. At least I think so. I have no statistical evidence for my position. Perhaps some exists; I really don't know. I draw my conclusions purely from anecdotal and experiential evidence. It convinces me.

People really can get Uncle Billy's temper along with his red hair.

We all know families where their children model, at least in the public realm, all the qualities we desire for our own brood. They're cheerful, instantly obedient, and look adults in the eye with a respectful smile on their faces. I've had the pleasure of knowing such a family. The children were a delight. The parents had done an excellent job raising them, and I was anxious for some inside tips. With the behavior of my crotchety toddler uppermost in my mind, I asked the mother if her children ever rebelled. She thought hard, obviously anxious to help me by relating to my question. Her countenance brightened;

she could relate. Yes, she knew what I was talking about. Her youngest had once said *no* to her.

I have always remembered that conversation. Not because I doubted the veracity of her words. I believe she was relating her experience honestly. I've remembered it because her experience was so different from mine. Why were things so different for them? It is certainly possible and likely that they had reared their children in a more consistent fashion than my husband and I had reared ours, although we certainly tried hard. But they had a distinct advantage over us. All their children had inherited mom and dad's gentle, cheerful nature. Our children were like us.

My husband and I are very different people. I come from a fairly large family, consisting primarily of girls. The give and take between us was direct. There was no subtlety, but no simmering resentments. Sometimes words were too sharp, but the barbs didn't go deep and were usually quickly forgotten. My husband's upbringing was very different. His family is much more gracious and careful of words. In fact, words of disagreement were rarely spoken. Confrontation was even rarer. When problems arose, the offender, through some secret osmosis that remains a mystery to me, was to correct the error without words or discussion.

When we married, we should have known instantly we were headed for trouble. Our perspectives on communication were so different. As my husband aptly states it, "Diana's motto is, 'If you love me you'll fight with me.' My motto is, 'If you love me you not only won't fight with me, you won't even talk about it!'" Through the years we have both had to modify our personalities, working towards a balance that has been good for both of us. However, we have been dismayed to find out our kids are just like us. We have two types of sinners at our house. We have in-your-face sinners and subtle, quiet sinners. They really do bear a remarkable resemblance to their parents.

Some of you were convinced from your own experience, before I presented any evidence, that personality traits are inherited. Your own brood has proven it to you time and time again. So what's my point? It is this: for those of you who have difficult children, don't see every struggle you face as a personal failure. You may be hoeing a harder row. (It may be the same hard row your parents hoed with you!) For those of you with children who have proven easy to raise, disperse grace freely on your sisters with greater struggles.

The Adam Effect

Besides Uncle Billy, another distant relative has had an even more profound effect on us. His name was Adam, and our resemblance to him is very striking indeed. He began a mess that even homeschooling can't straighten out. That is an important fact to remember. Sometimes we get lost in the warm fuzzy stories we tell and hear about homeschooling, but these stories represent a compilation of homeschool's finest moments, not the experiences of every waking hour. In our idealistic zeal we expect all to be sunshine and flowers. When there are clouds and weeds we feel like failures, believing it is somehow our fault. In one sense it is, but the problem is much bigger than our weaknesses alone.

In our idealistic zeal we expect all to be sunshine and flowers.

We are redeemed sinners living in a sinful world. We have chosen to homeschool, hoping to prevent some of the tarnish from rubbing off on our children. To some extent it works. To some extent it fails because the tarnish is not just around us, it is in us. Like the Apostle Paul, we can query, "O wretched man that I am! Who will deliver me from this body of death?" (Romans 7:24). We would all be appalled and stunned if someone shouted, "Homeschooling will!" Of course, we don't believe that, but our feelings sometimes state something different. We work so hard at what we are doing. We work so sincerely, so desirous of God's blessing. Surely we will be successful. Then difficulties begin. We feel we have done something wrong for our son to have such an attitude. We feel we have done something wrong if our youngest wakes up grumpy most mornings. We expect faithful homeschooling to prevent sin or failure from ever entering our door. When it doesn't, we are quick to accuse ourselves.

Sometimes we *have* done something wrong, and I am not in any way trying to justify our failures. Perhaps we have been negligent in our duties. We may have allowed bad attitudes to go unchallenged. Our little one may be crabby because we have been careless in enforcing bedtimes. If such is the case we should seek forgiveness, pick up the pieces, and start afresh.

Often, however, it is not our failure that is the problem, it is our expectations. We want results that defy our humanity. We want homeschooling to give us children who fill our every waking hour with obedience and good cheer. We want homeschooling to save us from the muck of this life. We want it to be our Messiah, our Christ.

Don't mar your homeschool efforts by expecting too much from them. Don't expect homeschooling to perfect your children. That is the lifework of Jesus Christ. Our efforts are a shoddy replacement at best. Know that we will always have struggles in this world. We will always sin, and so will our children. The final culmination of our redemption occurs in eternity, not in this life. At that time there will be great rejoicing.

And I heard a loud voice from heaven saying, "Behold, the tabernacle of God is with men, and He will dwell with them, and they shall be His people, and God Himself will be with them and be their God. And God will wipe away every tear from their eyes; there shall be no more death, nor sorrow, nor crying; and there shall be no more pain, for the former things have passed away." (Revelation 21:3-4)

Peace through the Struggle

Sometimes when we struggle with a difficult child we fail to keep a few thoughts in perspective. Let's look at a few ideas now. Perhaps they will help you sleep better at night.

First of all, we must recognize that our children are not our clones. Some of their decisions will reflect the training we have so carefully instilled in them. Other decisions will not. It is a great disillusionment to strive so hard and then see the fruit dashed to the ground and spoiled. Yet we must not berate ourselves for our children's individual decisions. It is our responsibility to be faithful to our calling; our children are responsible to be faithful to theirs. Still, we may feel guilty. Sometimes we should. Perhaps we have sinned towards our child. Guilt that leads to repentance is a blessing. Never be hesitant to ask a child's forgiveness. The resulting forgiveness heals relationships and provides a fresh beginning. It encourages accurate evaluation and constructive change. False guilt is a different matter. It nags us with the unsettled feeling that we have more control over our children's choices than we really do. It blames us for not being able to force change. It is not from God. It is trying to take the place of God.

Secondly, we must bear patiently with our children's immaturity. Remember that they are just beginning their spiritual pilgrimage. Sometimes we expect them to have the wisdom at fifteen that we are struggling to gain at forty. They are not finished products when their homeschooling years are over. In fact, they won't be finished products until eternity! As our influence diminishes we must pray that God in His mercy will be swift to draw individuals into their lives to encourage them in paths of righteousness.

Finally, so many of the problems we struggle over reach wonderful solutions through God's providence. I remember visiting with a father whose unmarried daughter had given his wife and him an unexpected grandchild. The initial shock and struggle were great. Tremendous lessons were learned. The grandchild is now the delight of their lives. God, in His providence, transformed their daughter's disobedience into glory. In His mercy He can turn even our greatest struggles into marvelous blessings.

My words, however kindly meant, cannot remove all the pain of wayward children. The feelings of failure can overwhelm us, especially because we know we are such imperfect models of what we desire our children to become. Let's look more closely at the solid hope and consolation found in God's Word and character.

Rich Comfort in God's Word

There is so much comfort in God's Word for the struggling parent or child, wonderful promises of tender forgiveness and watchful care. Let me point out just a few of its well-known treasures.

"Come now, and let us reason together," says the Lord, "Though your sins are like scarlet, they shall be as white as snow; though they are red like crimson, they shall be as wool." (Isaiah 1:18)

Behold! The Lamb of God who takes away the sin of the world! (John 1:29b)

If we confess our sins, He is faithful and just to forgive us our sins and to cleanse us from all unrighteousness. (I John 1:9)

I have also always found God's word to Israel, as spoken through the prophet Jeremiah, a great help. They had sinned greatly, had been unfaithful to God, and would soon be carried off into captivity to Babylon. But even in judgment God remembers mercy:

For I know the thoughts that I think toward you, says the Lord, thoughts of peace and not of evil, to give you a future and a hope. Then you will call upon Me and go and pray to Me, and I will listen to you. And you will seek Me and find Me, when you search for Me with all your heart. (Jeremiah 29:11-13)

These words were spoken to a rebellious people. They are a promise that if the people repented He would be swift to forgive and restore. They are wonderful words of restoration to share with a child struggling through the consequences of his sin.

Rich Comfort in God's Character

There is also great comfort in God's character for parent and child alike.

He is all-knowing. In His omniscience He knows us perfectly. Although our sinful natures sometime startle us, they never take Him by surprise.

He is all-wise. In the all-wise counsel of His will He chose to give our children to us. He had no illusions we would raise them perfectly. We are to do our best with His help, letting His grace cover the multitude of our sins.

He is all-powerful. No situation is beyond Him. Nothing leaves God wringing His hands. He is in control. We can safely trust in His power in the hardest of circumstances. He is our shepherd; we are His sheep. He watches over us from a position of strength.

We can never love our children more than their Savior does.

He is also infinitely good. No difficult situation will come our way that is not brought by the hand of a good God. In the here-and-now we may doubt the blessing, but in eternity we will know the greater good was always accomplished through our struggles.

All-knowing, all-wise, all-powerful, and infinitely good. To add glory to glory, He is perfect love. We can never love our children more than their Savior does. He loves His children with an intensity we cannot understand. It is so unfathomable it drove Him to the cross to secure our redemption. We know He loves His lambs with a love far surpassing our own in its perfection. However, that does not mean He will never allow our children to stumble. He does.

Being earthly parents, we sometimes consider our children's struggles to be evidence of our abject failure as parents. Do not forget their heavenly Father has been on watchcare duty over our children with us. He could have prevented all the difficulties, intervening dramatically, as He did on the Damascus road, or in quieter, subtler ways. Yet He has allowed their struggles. Are we as quick to condemn His parenting as we are our own? In the very deepest of despairing moments, we may. In our wiser moments we must trust in the goodness of His character.

God's vision is so far above ours. He sees both the beginning and the end. Our destinies, and those of our children, are culminated in eternity and God sees the path there clearly. We tend to be near-sighted, seeing only the obstacles immediately before our noses. The clarity of God's Word can be the comforting means by which we learn to see through our Father's eyes.

God's purposes are also above ours, and we will not always understand. Sometimes it will take great trials before a wayward child recognizes how desperately he needs the Lord. We may trust that no painful experience is wasted, for God in His love will use it all for our good and His glory.

It is during these difficult times of life that we realize how desperately we need our Savior. It is in deep difficulties that our faith is most real. The struggles drive us to our knees in fervent prayer. There is no better place to be.

Rich Comfort in God's People

When our children commit foolish deeds or sinful acts, it is natural for parents to seek advice or solace. The desire for support is especially great for homeschool mothers; we have invested so much of our lives into our children. But consolation must not be sought without discretion. Our children may be greatly harmed if we broadcast their failings in a heedless search for comfort and understanding. Working in the bookstore, I have at times listened with great discomfort to a litany of a child's shortcomings while junior took in every word. Fortunately, I have also been blessed to witness great parental love and tact when dealing with a struggling child. Respect your children's privacy. Their failings are their pain, too. If the problem is of a sinful nature, a transgression that is made too public can make a child feel that he can never again enjoy the respect of others. Share your child's struggles discretely with those who love him and will pray for him or with those in a position to help him.

One of the best blessings in our life has been our church family. They have been of priceless value. Different individuals have initiated personal relationships with our children. They have prayed for them. They have parented with us. They have shown the love of Christ to children who have not always been easy to love. At times they have provided a fresh voice speaking the same truths, somehow making them more palatable in the process. They have illustrated the depth and breadth of the Christian faith. They have lived out the truth of the Gospel and made it real. It is how the body of Christ is designed to function. This living out of gospel love is especially important when the problem is of a sinful nature. When children struggle, parents often receive the brunt of their unhappiness. In the crisis of the moment children may reject parental values. They may also reject their parents' faith. At times like this a praying, loving church family is of infinite value.

Wayward children need to see the enormity of the Christian faith—that it is not just some crazy philosophical aberration of their parents, to be accepted or rejected on a capricious whim. They must see that the gospel is much bigger than the faith of their parents—that it is indeed the vital lifeblood of all humanity. This can be *learned* by introducing our students to their forefathers in the faith through the study of church history. This is *experienced* through years of relationship building with God's people.

Parents need great support at these times, also. They need a place of refuge where they will be comforted and accepted. They need a place of safe reflection where counsel and encouragement and gentle admonitions, when necessary, can be offered. What opportunities we have to minister to each other!

How blessed we are if we have a Christian support system for our times of greatest trial. If we don't, we must pray that God will open that opportunity for us. Such prayer is time well spent.

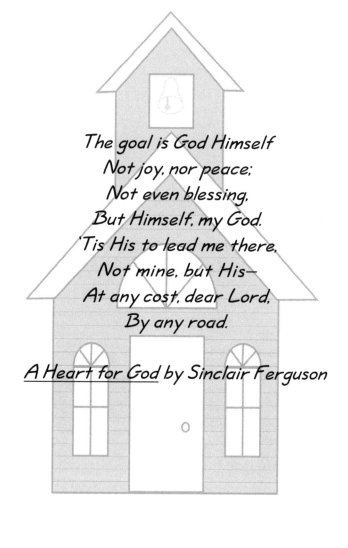

The goal is God Himself
Not joy, nor peace;
Not even blessing,
But Himself, my God.
'Tis His to lead me there,
Not mine, but His—
At any cost, dear Lord,
By any road.

A Heart for God by Sinclair Ferguson

Looking Towards Eternity

I was not a Christian when I was a child, although I believe God's hand was upon me creating a yearning in my heart for Him. In my teen years I heard the gospel clearly explained for the first time and answered its compelling call. My early college years were a time of great zeal. I arranged my class schedule carefully, making sure I had an hour in my dorm room each day for Bible reading and prayer. I attended organized missionary prayer times most evenings. I saturated my life in prayer. I was a new Christian on fire.

Life moved on, I married, and babies came. Once toddlers outgrew regular naptimes I discovered that scheduling daily time with the Lord had lost its simplicity. I suffered great pangs of guilt. A book I read added to my dilemma. It recommended setting my alarm to have devotions at 2:00 or 3:00 a.m. while the household was still and peaceful. It worked well for the author. It was a prescription for physical collapse for an exhausted mother of energetic toddlers. In a season of life when using the restroom in privacy was an unheard of luxury, I struggled to find my needed time with the Lord.

As my children continue to grow and the cares and activities of life change and multiply, maintaining a quiet time with the Lord remains one of my most challenging ongoing struggles. I have gone so far as to occasionally wish we were back in medieval times with the Bible chained to the pulpit. You can't be held accountable for neglect under such circumstances!

At times I have yearned for the simple college days of unfettered spiritual abandon. If I'm honest, however, there were some undesirable characteristics to my fervor. I was so *me* centered. Although I often prayed fervently for missionaries, I spent just as much time bombarding heaven over embarrassingly selfish personal desires. I was zealous, but it was often a self-centered zeal without wisdom.

At times I have yearned for the simple college days of unfettered spiritual abandon.

God is Faithful

The years have passed, filled with great joys and great struggles. I can see that I have changed. Amazingly, I *have* grown spiritually. My wisdom *has* increased. This is most emphatically *not* due to an ability to pull myself up by my own spiritual bootstraps—I tripped over the laces long ago. It is the undeserved blessing of a faithful God who is always true to His nature. He has promised to make me one with Him and to conform me to His image. He unswervingly stays that eternal course while I flit after the elusive butterflies of this life. I am faithless. He is faithful. All praise to His glorious name!

What am I saying? When Paul asks in Romans 6:1 if we should continue in sin so grace may abound, would I respond with a hearty "Amen?" Of course not. If we are alive in Christ we are to die to sin. But it is so much easier to say than do. As a very weak and wobbly pilgrim, my hope *must* lie in the sufficiency of Christ's sacrifice and His ability to keep me eternally.

Bringing Glory to God

As wives, moms, and homeschool teachers, we have many and varied tasks—we have just spent a whole book looking at them! A ceaseless parade of duties demands our attention. Our focus is drawn to this life, and we lose our eternal perspective. Yet we have one overarching purpose that far surpasses every other task set before us, even homeschooling: we are to bring glory to God. To accomplish this we must faithfully use the means of grace God has given us—the activities He has appointed which work actively in our lives to conform us to Himself.

Some Means of God's Grace in Our Lives

We must study God's Word. The scope of its benefits are beyond measure. It is righteous and faithful. It is a lamp to our feet and a light to our path. It gives understanding to the simple. It preserves us from sin. It gives us great peace when we abide in its wisdom. It is the joy and rejoicing of our hearts. It endures forever. What peril we place ourselves and our children in when we neglect its wise guidance through this life!

We must pray. If we desire fellowship with God, we must seek out His presence, both privately and corporately. Heartfelt private prayer allows us to share with our Father the deepest recesses of our soul. Corporate prayer knits God's people together in bonds of love. Both private and corporate prayer make us increasingly aware of our humble dependence on the Lord for everything in our lives. Answered prayer uplifts the heart and blesses the soul. It reveals God's tender hand on our lives. It causes us to rejoice in His blessings and gives us confidence in God's goodness as we endure trial.

We must not forsake the assembling of the brethren together. Salvation is not only a private matter. We are saved into the Body of Christ to love and serve fellow believers. We draw strength from one another. We have been gifted to meet one another's needs. We glean godly wisdom. We share joys and tears. We triumph over struggles. By contrast the path alone is a fearsome one. "But woe to him who is alone when he falls, for he has no one to help him up" (Ecclesiastes 4: 10b). Let us choose the path of fellowship and servanthood for the good of our souls.

The Blessings of Faithfulness

What a privilege to worship a God who is unchangeable in His love for His people! When we fail to see God's hand on our lives it is because of failings in us, not in Him. Sometimes, like shallow ground, we initially rejoice in our faith but fail to root deeply in the

Lord, letting the urgencies of life draw our attention away from what is eternal. The fact that we struggle to maintain Bible reading, prayer, and spiritually meaningful fellowship is a chief indicator of their worth. Temptation does not pull us away from the useless or valueless; temptation pulls us away from what is precious and irreplaceable.

When we utilize the means of grace God has given us, our faithfulness to God joins with His constancy towards us. The relationship is full and strong and yields priceless fruit. We will see God bless us in ways we had not expected because our hearts will be tuned to see the evidence of His abiding presence. Such awareness transforms our lives.

We will recognize that we are not alone. Life has many blessings, but it is during the struggles that our friendship with God is priceless beyond measure. Several years ago, due to circumstances beyond our control, we found ourselves in a very serious financial situation. We feared that we would lose our home and that I would have to go to work full time. Our entire way of life was threatened, including our ability to continue homeschooling. Resolution of the crisis took months. Despite the stress and nights broken with sleeplessness, it was a time of blessing. I prayed with a fervency and clutched Scripture with a tenacity that cheerier times hadn't inspired in me. I was ever watchful for the hand of God and I prayed daily for His intervention. He did not disappoint me. I saw dramatic answers that excited my faith. But just as important, I was gently prodded to see the quiet evidences of His presence. My hunger for God, brought on by trial, was teaching me about the peace that passeth all understanding and providing a deep assurance that God is good.

We will recognize that all of life is lived in the light of eternity. This recognition can illuminate the way we live our lives. Everyday tasks, including our homeschooling, become sacred when they are faithfully performed to the glory of God. Even our smallest duties provide a preparation in finite time for eternity, when all of creation will be renewed to serve God in perfect love. We also recognize that everyday irritants have their eternal purposes. From the misplaced schoolbook to the driver who daydreams in the left turn lane so that we must wait through another light sequence, all aggravations are meant to encourage growth in Christ-like righteousness. God wastes no experiences in His pursuit of our sanctification. Embracing life's duties and small struggles as purposeful and from our loving Father's hand insures that God will be glorified whether we eat or drink or whatsoever we do.

We will recognize the ultimate goal. The temporal blessings which God lavishes on us are precious. Yet they pale in comparison to the most exalted blessing of all, *His priceless friendship.* The pearl beyond price is the growth in oneness with our Savior. The goal is God Himself, at any cost, by any road.

O God beyond all praising,
We worship you today
And sing the love amazing
That songs cannot repay;
For we can only wonder
At every gift you send,
At blessings without number
And mercies without end:
We lift our hearts before you
And wait upon your word,
We honor and adore you,
Our great and mighty Lord.

Then hear, O gracious Savior,
Accept the love we bring,
That we who know your favor
May serve you as our King,
And whether our tomorrows
Be filled with good or ill,
We'll triumph through our sorrows
And rise to bless you still:
To marvel at your beauty
And glory in your ways,
And make a joyful duty
Our sacrifice of praise.

(Michael Perry, 1982, Hymn 660 in the *Trinity Hymnal,* revised edition, 1990)

Epilogue (That means closing section; can you hide your eyes and spell it?)

Well, here we are at the end of the book. It's time for me to pack my bag and head back home. We've covered quite a bit, haven't we? I can't know how my words have affected you, but I know what I desire.

I hope you are more comfortable with your family's uniqueness. It is the flowering of your distinctives in submission to Christ that will bring the greatest glory to God.

I hope it is easier for you to plan a homeschool program that fits your needs. Do what works. Use your creativity to celebrate your special talents.

I hope you are encouraged to control your life and choose your areas of excellence. When it is fine for something to just be okay, let that be okay with you.

I hope you have found some scheduling help for your situation. As you strive to bring order to your daily existence, remain flexible. Some of the most precious and blessed moments of life spring from its many interruptions.

I hope the next time your child misbehaves you will not die from terminal embarrassment and discouragement. They all sin. Mine do too. Let's turn our emotional energy to the throne of grace and pray each other through the challenge.

I hope you have laughed at yourself. We do it far too seldom.

I hope you have realized that life can be lived both spiritually and pragmatically. The two approaches are not at cross purposes, but blend quite nicely.

I hope you will encourage love for other home, private, or public schoolers. We are all in such need of grace!

I hope you will cease activity long enough to love well those most precious to you.

Most importantly, I hope you have been brought anew to where your true worth lies. It is in the palms of Our Lord's nail-pierced hands.

A Postscript to the Epilogue (if there is such a thing)

I just talked to my youngest daughter. Her new room is wonderful, her carpet is sooo soft, and it's okay that I went away. Tonight, when we read, we will get those children home from their camping trip. It's a good thing, too. I think rain is predicted for tomorrow.

Also by Diana Johnson

Home-Designed High School

ISBN: 0971073406
Suggested Retail: 22.95
Pages: 208
Size: 8 1/2 by 11
Binding: lay flat perfect binding

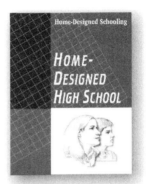

Home-Designed High School is a user-friendly guide to preparing your homeschool high schooler for college admissions. Its timely information will help you understand college entrance requirements, create the optimum high school program for your student, keep appropriate records, credit and grade courses, compile a transcript, calculate a GPA, and more! Read how homeschoolers have reviewed *Home-Designed High School:*

> "[Mrs. Johnson's] book is a full size gentle walk through everything that you really need to know about designing and documenting your student's high school experience...Simply, you can't go wrong with this book."-*Pam Stauter*, NYS Loving Education at Home

> "Thank you, Diana Johnson!!! Whew. Breathe. This is how I am feeling now that I have finally found a resource to calm my 'high-school-teaching-jittery-nerves.' Transcripts, computing GPA's, yearly study plans, college planning, keeping track of credits, requirements for college entrance—as I pored over page after information-packed page, I could actually picture myself sitting down with this calm wonderful communicator over a cup of tea feeling the 'high school stress' wash away. Diana Johnson, in her *Home-Designed High School*, does an uncannily great job of anticipating the reader's panic. She is able to put things into perspective, offering hope, common sense, and gentle reminders that the entire high school homeschool adventure is meant to glorify God and need not be overwhelming." -Product review by *Jenefer Igarashi*, Senior Editor, *The Old Schoolhouse Magazine*

Also by Diana Johnson

The Starting Point

Suggested Retail: 2.95
Size: 5 1/2 by 8 1/2
Pages: 52

Although *The Starting Point* is just a small, inexpensive booklet, it can be a big help! As a new homeschooler, you will find it provides answers to many of your most important questions. Contents include:

- the benefits of homeschooling
- the responsibilities of homeschooling
- types of curriculum
- deciding what type of curriculum is best for you
- record-keeping and grading
- staying sane
- teaching with little ones in the home
- teaching teens
- addresses for national organizations
- recommended reading

The Starting Point is available at your local Christian bookstore's homeschool department,
or you may e-mail
homedesignedschooling@cox-internet.com

(distributed to bookstores through Appalachian Distributors)